Echoes of October

Echoes of October

International Commemorations of the Bolshevik Revolution 1918–1990

EDITORS:

Jean-François Fayet, Valérie Gorin
and Stefanie Prezioso

Part of the Studies in Twentieth Century Communism Series

Series Editors: Norman LaPorte, Kevin Morgan
and Matthew Worley

Lawrence & Wishart
London 2017

Lawrence and Wishart Limited
Central Books Building
Freshwater Road
Chadwell Heath
RM8 1RX

© Lawrence & Wishart 2017
Individual articles © author

The authors have asserted their rights under the Copyright, Design and Patents Act, 1998 to be identified as the authors of this work.

All rights reserved. Apart from fair dealing for the purpose of private study, research, criticism or review, no part of this publication may be reproduced, stored in a retrieval system, or transmitted, in any form or by any means, electronic, electrical, chemical, mechanical, optical, photocopying, recording or otherwise, without the prior permission of the copyright owner.

ISBN 9781910448960

British Library Cataloguing in Publication Data.
A catalogue record for this book is available from the British Library

Typesetting: e-type
Cover design: Andrew Corbett
Cover image: Bibliothèque de Documentation Internationale Contemporaine (BDIC): France-URSS, 1967 R.

Contents

Series Editors' Foreword 1

Jean-François Fayet, Preface 6

1. **Eric Aunoble,** Commemorating an Event That Never Occurred: Russia's October in Soviet Ukraine in the 1920s 28

2. **Ottokar Luban,** The Echoes of the Russian October under the State of Siege in Germany, October/November 1918 56

3. **Kasper Braskén,** Celebrating October: The Transnational Commemorations of the Tenth Anniversary of the Soviet Union in Weimar Germany 76

4. **Daniel Kowalsky,** Exporting Soviet Commemoration: The Spanish Civil War and the October Revolution, 1936-1939 106

5. **Anastasia Koukouna,** Commemorating the October Revolution in Greece, 1918-1949 135

6. **André Liebich,** The Mensheviks Commemorate October 160

7. **Stephan Rindlisbacher,** The Echoes of the Echoes: Reflecting the International Commemoration of the October Revolution in the Newspaper *Pravda*, 1918-91 177

Notes on Contributors 196

Index 198

Series Editors' Foreword

Describing the French revolution as the founding moment of the nineteenth century, Eric Hobsbawm maintained that it was so universally regarded as such that a key dimension of the history of the revolution was what the nineteenth century made of it. As Hobsbawm would have been the first to acknowledge, for most of the twentieth century, the same was true of the Bolshevik revolution of November 1917. If the nineteenth century, in other words, had variously 'studied, copied, compared itself to, or tried to avoid, bypass, repeat, or go beyond the French Revolution', the Russian revolution served as exactly such a reference point and bone of contention for the century that followed.[1] Indeed, the immediacy of the issue was in many respects incomparably greater in the twentieth century, in that the Russian revolution, unlike the French, was for decades thereafter continuously embodied in a party, state and global political movement, which traced their origins to the revolution and claimed to uphold its legacy. For large parts of Hobsbawm's short twentieth century, this was the defining issue of international politics, and often, depending on the time and place, of domestic politics too.[2]

What the twentieth century made of October — the shorthand name for the revolution that communists continued to derive from the pre-revolutionary Russian calendar — is therefore a rich field of study in itself. Through the institutionalisation of its legacy in state and party, there was, from the start, a culture of official commemoration. In the French case, this only has any durable parallels when the Third Republic became established after 1871.

Even then, the annual celebration of the falling of the Bastille was of far more limited international resonance, with commemorations mostly in France itself. The Bolshevik revolution, by contrast, was not only commemorated on a large scale internationally, but beyond the reach of the party-states of the Eastern bloc; this gave rise to forms of political rivalry and ideological contestation between different movements and parties taking their own distinct positions on the legacy of October. As Jean-François Fayet describes in this volume, the commemoration of October had the important function of marking out the 'territory of the comrades'; but at the same time it was always a contested territory and October itself was the occasion for rival appropriations, critical commentary and attempted delegitimation.

As the revolution on its centenary once more provides the focus of extensive media interest and public comment, it is therefore fitting that the journal *Twentieth Century Communism* turns its attention to the politics of commemoration itself. It does so by publishing papers presented at the conference on 'The International Echoes of the Commemorations of the October Revolution (1918-1990)' held at the University of Lausanne in September 2016 and co-sponsored by the journal. While for the most part, the echoes discussed were European ones, the papers were of the scope and quality for both a themed issue of the journal, appearing in the autumn of 2017, and this separate volume in the journal's new book series, Studies in Twentieth Century Communism. The introduction, by the project's initiator Jean-François Fayet, appears in both publications; the journal contains further papers from the conference on the contested commemorations of the Cold War years.[3] The chapters presented here, meanwhile, focus on the three decades or so immediately following the Russian revolution, or what, following Fernando Claudin, we might characterise as the period 'From Comintern to Cominform'.[4]

SERIES EDITORS' FOREWORD

The chapters in this volume range from the physical territories of Soviet Ukraine and exiled oppositionists in the shape of the Mensheviks to the broader international agencies with which Willi Münzenberg's name is synonymous and the communist parties in Germany, Spain and Greece that were actively engaged in Hobsbawm's 'secular struggle' between the old and the new. Within the limits of its period and European focus, the collection thus takes us through a series of shifting contexts. Together, these chapters offer fresh perspectives on the interplay of national and international, which features prominently in the communist historiography of these decades. In his reflections on the communist movement in the first issue of *Twentieth Century Communism*, Bernhard Bayerlein identified the movement's 'nationalisation' as a central feature of the period covered here, with the USSR's transformation into an imagined 'Workers' Fatherland'.[5] The echoes of October invite further consideration of this development in respect of two implicit tensions or ambiguities. The first was the tension between October as a process of revolutionary change, still requiring re-enactment and thus completion on an international scale, and its identification with the state institutions to which it had given rise, and whose safeguarding was thus established as the revolutionary worker's highest duty. While it was fundamental to the mystique of proletarian internationalism that no contradiction was formally admissible between the interests of the Soviet state and those of revolutionary workers within and beyond its borders, the chapters presented here document very clearly how these considerations shaped the commemoration of October internationally.

At the same time, the very nature of the Russian epithet 'October' seemed to imply a revolution whose decisive breakthrough was of a national character. In France, it was the deepening of the revolution that liberals contrived to sidestep when they marked out 1789 from 1792 or 1793. In the case of

October, the cult of 1917 was fundamentally a reflection of the failure of any other revolutionary movement to establish itself in power. By the same token, however, it also offered scope for the abstraction of the revolution from the broader convulsions and solidarity actions within which it must be located. Within the USSR, as Eric Aunoble describes here, the result in Ukraine was the commemoration of an event that 'never occurred' and the framing of October within a long-term narrative in which Ukraine's particularities might equally be included or forgotten. From a broader Soviet perspective, Stefan Rindlisbacher locates the crucial turn to a fundamentally national narrative towards the end of the 1930s. But there is also scope for further work on the commemorative calendars of other communist parties and of the communist movement internationally, and on the extent to which the precepts of socialism in one country had been prefigured from an early date by the commemoration of the revolution in one country.

The present collection maps out an important field of study, but it is a field that as yet is in its relative infancy; the book and journal issue together constitute an important contribution to our understanding of the communist politics of memory. The editors of the Studies in Twentieth Century Communism series are therefore greatly indebted to Jean-François Fayet, Stéfanie Prezioso and Valérie Gorin for both proposing and editing these publications and (along with Korine Amacher) acting as principal organisers of the conference from which they derive. Norman LaPorte and Kevin Morgan represented the journal at the conference and also assisted with editing and language issues in the book and journal. Acknowledgement should also be made of the support received from the Swiss National Foundation and the University of Lausanne which made the conference possible; and both organisers and editors would like to thank Katharine Harris at Lawrence & Wishart for her special care in seeing the book chapters through to publication. Appearing alongside the inaugural volume of the series on *Weimar Communism as Mass Movement*, the chapters presented here confirm once more the importance of such transnational collaborations and we trust that they will prove to be the first of many.

NOTES

1. Eric Hobsbawm, *Echoes of the Marseillaise. Two centuries look back on the French revolution*, Verso: London, 1989, pxi, p69.
2. For Hobsbawm's observations, see his *Age of Extremes: The short twentieth century 1914-1991*, Michael Joseph: London, 1994, ch. 2.
3. Journal articles include: Virgile Cirefice, *Celebrating the Russian revolution? A socialist dilemma. France, Italy, 1945-1956*; Jesper Jørgensen, *The Commemorations of the October Revolution in Denmark during the Cold War – a marker of radicalism?*; Matteo Bertelé, *Venice 1977: (Counter)celebrations of the October Revolution*; Alexander Höbel, *Anniversaries of the October Revolution in the political-cultural magazine of the Italian Communist Party: Rinascita, 1957-1987*; Valérie Gorin, *The journalist as a foreign expert – American TV correspondents reporting on the November parades (1960s-1980s)*.
4. Fernando Claudin, *The Communist Movement: from Comintern to Cominform*, Penguin: Harmondsworth, 1975.
5. Bernhard H. Bayerlain, 'Collisions of cultures and nationalism as patterns of the "Soviet century"', *Twentieth Century Communism*, 1, 2009, 160-3.

Preface

> It is necessary (for purely political reasons) to demonstrate to the diplomats and to members of the Communist International the strength of the Republic and the faith the masses of workers have in Soviet power.
>
> Telegram from Leon Trotsky to the Central Committee of the Russian Communist Party[1]

> My only consolation is that as celebrations are bourgeois institutions at which nobody tells the truth it is perhaps just as well that I shall be at a safe distance.
>
> Letter from George Bernard Shaw to Polovtseva[2]

First of all, there was the Revolution. Then the myth took over from reality. The October Revolution became a celebration; then, a succession of commemorative celebrations.[3] A set of controlled memories, made up of symbols, rites and beliefs, these October celebrations fulfilled, like all commemorations, three main functions: bringing together, legitimising, and mobilising.

As a symbol, the October celebrations first of all contributed to the formation of a shared community. According to Anatoly Lunacharsky, the main theoretician of Soviet commemorative rituals, the celebrations were 'the art that is closest to revolution', because they brought the masses together, making them feel proud and sure of themselves. Thus, people feel 'that they live as a people and not like a sack of potatoes knocking into one another'.⁴ The transfigured, collective 'us' also had its oppositional counterpart in the celebrations, in the demonised image of the enemy, whose omnipresent threat reinforced the need for unity. As integral parts of the revolutionary arts, the celebrations were also one of the main vectors of political propaganda.

The second function of the October commemorations was to legitimise, to transmit an explanation for and a representation of power.⁵ Through the celebrations, which were the preferred location of discourse, power was demonstrated to the masses, and the interpretation of history by those in power was transmitted to the people. In producing a legitimising interpretation of the present, the commemorations ultimately constituted part of the transformation that was in progress. As militant celebrations, the October commemorations served the cause by declaring the objectives of the regime and mobilising the masses to face the struggles yet to come. Each October anniversary thus presented a variation on remembrance, which was updated by the changing national and international contexts over time.

In addition to their domestic role in fostering unity, providing legitimacy, and facilitating internal mobilisation, commemoration practices also supported the regime's international eminence, especially when it presented itself as a model for world revolution. From the earliest years, the choreography of October commemorations involved consideration for the gaze of the outside world in the organisation of the celebrations. This willingness to give the October commemorations an international echo was manifested in three ways: the first was the participation of foreigners in the celebrations taking place in the Soviet Union. As an allegory of the people marching towards revolution, the 7 November march had to reflect the solidarity of the international proletariat with October. The second international echo was in broadcasting the celebrations in the foreign media: this was the media echo of October. The press, the radio, and the newsreels, and later the television broadcasts enabled the circulation of the celebratory spectacle, and amplified the celebrations in the USSR and outside it. The third international echo was the organisation of commemorative events outside Soviet borders, thus extending the territory of October. The commemoration of the Russian Revolution of 1917 was not merely a Soviet event.

PARTICIPATION OF FOREIGNERS IN THE 7 NOVEMBER COMMEMORATIONS IN THE USSR

Inviting foreign dignitaries to National Day celebrations is a tradition as old as diplomacy itself. However, assisted by the communist parties, the trade unions, and the cultural organisations, the Soviets took this tradition to a whole new level. This unusual feature was quantitatively manifested in the number of guests, and qualitatively in the techniques used to select them. These techniques were concerned with political marketing, and particularly focused on the concept of a representative panel.

During the years of civil war, only a few non-Soviet delegates attended the celebrations. They were almost exclusively foreign communists living in Russia, such as the Frenchman Pierre Pascal who took part in the march.[6] With the New Economic Policy and the first diplomatic recognition, the numbers of foreigners visiting the USSR increased significantly, and there were several dozen of them in the commemorations of 1921 and 1922. The first attempt to give the event a truly international dimension was in 1923,[7] but this sixth anniversary commemoration was a failure because most of the communist machinery had been mobilised elsewhere by the organisation of an uprising in Germany. The subsequent commemorations over the next three years had little more non-Soviet participation.

But in 1927, a thousand foreign delegates, from forty-three different countries, were invited to the Soviet Union for the tenth anniversary of the revolution.[8] Around 80 per cent of them were workers. In addition to the trade union delegates and the representatives of the main factories, there were also guests from the Mezhrabpom (the International Workers Relief), the MOPR (International Red Aid), the cooperative movement, the peasant movement, representatives of proletarian defence organisations, proletarian sports associations, proletarian cyclists, proletarian Esperantists, proletarian Free Thinkers, proletarian stamp collectors, proletarian Friends of the Theatre and tenant unions. The most important national delegations in terms of numbers were the German, British, French, and Czechoslovakian delegations. The others were mainly representatives of the 'nationalist-revolutionary movements of the oppressed and colonised countries': the Nehru family, Sun Yat-sen's widow, the Turkish Foreign Minister, representatives from Nepal, Mongolia, Algeria (Mira Ali), Mexico, Argentina, Brazil, and Sierra Leone. Most of these delegations had been invited by The League Against Colonial Oppression. Finally, there were the members of the Western progressive intelligentsia, such as the writers Henri Barbusse, Theodore Dreiser, Panaït Istrati, Nikos Kazantzakis, the Japanese poet Ujaku Akita, and Gabrielle Duchêne of the Women's International League for Peace and Freedom.[9] Romain Rolland and Ernst Toller could not come, but they had sent letters of congratulation, which were published in the Soviet press. Only a few of these foreign delegates observed the official parade from the Red Square; the majority were organised into district columns inside the march.[10] Unlike the ambassadors, these representatives of the international working class and progressive social forces were not passive spectators, though their status was ambiguous. Despite having been invited as observers, they were expected to take sides, and then to commit themselves, because they had a role in the October spectacle and its political uses. The Soviets intended to show the world that the USSR was not isolated, and that its international legitimacy extended beyond the limited gamut of its diplomatic relations.

The invitation of foreigners on such a large scale relied on complex organisation. Starting with the tenth anniversary, and according to a plan drawn up by Willi Münzenberg,[11] this organisation served as a model for several decades. Matters related to the composition, invitation, and funding of the delegations were officially entrusted to a special international commission made up of representatives of various institutions: the Foreign Relations Committee of the Trade Unions (KVS-VTsSPS), the All-Union Society for Cultural Relations Abroad (VOKS), the Communist Youth International (KIM), and the Comintern (CI).[12] However, 'a large part of the campaign was left up to the initiative of Münzenberg and organisations influenced by him'.[13] According to the international commission, a foreign delegation should ideally be made up of 20 per cent Communists, 40 per cent Social Democrats and 40 per cent without party affiliation. The invitations were given based on the theory of distance formulated by Münzenberg in a circular sent to the CPs:

> To give this campaign for the sending of delegations to the USSR the broadest possible dimension, it is advisable for the first calls, the first manifestations to come from organisations, groups, people, and newspapers located as far as possible from the Communist movement. ... Because the organisation of the wave of solidarity in favour of the USSR should always be of a non-party nature in public.[14]

Münzenberg also insisted somewhat on the representativeness of delegates: by how many people had they been elected? In a factory containing how many workers? The clever percentages drafted in theory for the composition of the delegations proved difficult to maintain in practice due to the large number of refusals, especially from socialists who feared expulsion from their organisations. There were also those who feared, often correctly, that they would lose their jobs. This would become even more of a challenge for recruiting international delegates during the Cold War. In 1927, many prominent intellectual or artistic figures, such as Upton Sinclair, John Dewey, Albert Einstein, George Bernard Shaw, and H.G. Wells, also declined the invitation to the celebrations. Others were physically prevented from attending, like the Mayor of Calcutta (Sen Gupta) whose papers were confiscated by the British authorities. Meanwhile, agitators, militant anarchists or Trotskyites, and even some fascists, attempted to infiltrate the delegations.

As soon as they crossed the border, the delegates were the Soviets' full responsibility. The commission for the preparation of the tenth anniversary celebrations brought together the representatives of the committees for the celebrations from the main republics and those responsible for the various technical and artistic commissions. Collectively, they worked for months on creating successful celebrations and designing the welcome for the delegations. Everything had been meticulously prepared: from the decoration of the borders, railway stations, towns, and factories to the preparation of the 'spontaneous' welcome committees to checking tourist itineraries, supplying tickets for the shows, and refurbishing the hotels.[15] The translator-guides who accompanied the delegations during their stay were given special training. Unlike their foreign colleagues, with whom they shared an occupation, 'Soviet guides could not', wrote the head of the guides department, 'be content to be mere technical informers, living Baedekers'.[16] In addition to their language skills, they were ideological filters, which explained why the Soviets were not too happy if delegations brought their own translators with them. The delegations' two-week stay was not intended as a pleasure trip; they had not been invited as tourists, but to work, to investigate from Arkhangelsk to Yerevan, passing through Kharkov.[17] The visits and discussions took place according to a well-known system. Questions were passed on in advance to the Soviets who gave general replies designed to avoid embarrassing discussions about strikes, unemployment, differences in salary, and the police system. After spending two weeks travelling around the USSR, most of the delegates returned to Moscow to attend the celebrations in Red Square. It was also the Soviets, assisted by the Department of Agitation and Propaganda of the Communist International, who chose the slogans that were written on the banners of the foreign marchers. On their return to their respective countries, many of them were encouraged to carry out lecture tours and to publish enthusiastic reports about their journey.[18] The echo of the celebrations was thus heard outside the USSR for several months subsequent to the actual events.

Despite some adaptations, particularly stricter supervision of foreigners during their stay in the USSR, and enhanced monitoring on their return, the techniques and structures set up for the tenth anniversary subsequently underwent little change. After the peak in 1927, the number of foreign representatives invited to the USSR was limited to just a few hundred for the anniversaries over the next ten years. While the overall number of invitees remained relatively stable, there are nonetheless significant variations by country according to what was happening at an international level. During the years of the Great Depression, the largest delegations came from countries that were in crisis. They were made up of many unemployed people and highlighted the discrimination suffered by women and ethnic minorities, such as in the workers' delegation from the United States in 1931. From a political point of view, the Chinese, as victims of imperialism, took the place of honour. In 1936, and especially in 1937, the Spanish delegation occupied a special place in the parade, due to the support provided by the Soviet Union to the Republic during the Civil War that began in 1936.[19]

However, international delegates to the October commemorations became increasingly rare during the Great Terror, before disappearing altogether during the Great Patriotic War. In a context marked by international tensions and then by the Second World War, the commemorative parade reinforced its military and patriotic component. Far from the internationalist ambition of the first few anniversaries, the commemorations were now reduced to a display of Soviet military power.

After 1945, it became standard to invite the ambassadors posted to Moscow, the heads of friendly states from Europe and Asia, and the leaders of communist parties to the celebrations. On the thirtieth anniversary, the members of the foreign diplomatic and consular bodies, ministers, including the leader of the Finnish government, and representatives of cultural associations from Bulgaria, Poland, and Yugoslavia, attended an official reception organised by the Ministry of Foreign Affairs. The invitees traced the contours of, and the fluctuations in, Soviet foreign policy.[20] The beginning of the 1950s marked the development of Soviet influence in the Middle East and Latin America. Conversely, the disappearance of the Yugoslav communists from Red Square illustrated the schism of the years 1948-1953. The Soviets also took advantage of this concentration of communist leaders to organise political meetings outside the celebrations. Thus, as a prolongation of the fortieth anniversary, a meeting of Cominform was held in Moscow in the presence of CP leaders from twelve socialist countries, including Mao, Ho Chi Minh, Enver Hoxha, Todor Zhivkov, Janos Kadar, Walter Ulbricht, and Vladislav Gomulka.[21] Communist party leaders from fifty-six capitalist countries were also included in the group. It was during the 7 November celebrations that Khrushchev staged the reconciliation with Yugoslavia and the end of the Cuban missile crisis. In the 1960s, Red Square became an almost obligatory passageway for the representatives of the 'progressive' movements of the

'Third World'. The Vietnamese were the most regular visitors, but there were also Ethiopians, Somalis, and others. Meanwhile, the Chinese, who were very well-represented there during the 1950s, disappeared completely from the guest list, as did the Albanians. Also at this time, women and young people began to take a more central role in the parade. The Young Communist Organisation ran 'friendship trains', transport which enabled thousands of young people from the people's democracies to visit the Soviet Union during the celebrations.[22] Despite this attempt to display youth, the 1960s celebrations actually highlighted the stagnation of the regime and its ageing leaders.

In 1977, the sixtieth anniversary parade was watched from the grandstand by over a hundred foreign delegations from left-wing organisations, joined by the heads of state of communist countries. The number of attendees remained high for the seventieth anniversary a decade later and until the last commemoration, in 1990.

The foreign diplomatic corps traditionally attended National Day celebrations, but it was when they were absent that attracted most attention. In 1956, the representatives of the NATO countries boycotted the October commemorations in Moscow, to protest against the Soviet invasion of Hungary. The same happened from 1980 to 1982 because of the invasion of Afghanistan. The commemorative ceremonies were always a component of the international diplomatic game.

THE ECHO OF THE CELEBRATIONS IN FOREIGN MEDIA

This staging of the regime took advantage, right from the early years, of the technological revolutions that took place in the mass media throughout the twentieth century. The illustrated press, the radio, the newsreels that preceded the film in cinemas, and later the television, enabled circulation of the spectacle of the celebrations within the USSR and outside it.[23] It was with the mass media, capable of reaching audiences that were not physically present, that 'commemoration' in terms of 'remembering together' took on its full meaning. In this respect, the media significantly contributed to the international echo of October.

In contrast, the foreign general press – both daily and weekly newspapers – mainly cold-shouldered the event, apart from covering the jubilees and a few topical high points. However, from the 1920s onwards, the Soviet Union had its own publishing network (publishing houses, printing works, subscriber societies), which worked to transmit images and descriptions of the October commemorations around the world. These initially included Soviet publications translated into foreign languages, including explicitly commemorative publications: history books, published on the occasion of the jubilees,[24] small thematic leaflets that summarised ten, twenty, or fifty years of socialist enlightenment, and collections of speeches. There were also special editions of the main Soviet journals, which were translated into foreign languages: *The Newsletter of Information from the Society for Cultural Relations with Foreign Countries; The New Soviets; USSR in Construction,* and the *Moscow Daily News.*

The publishing system also produced communist publications that had been edited outside the Soviet Union. International communist party organisations took part each year in the commemorative mobilisation campaigns.[25] They reproduced the history series, the messages of congratulations from their delegations, and the main commemorative speeches. Publishers translated a number of Soviet authors, politicians, artists, and scholars.

The echo of the celebrations could also be heard in so-called 'non-party publications', which were nonetheless sympathetic to the communists or the USSR. Those most suited to the event were the illustrated newspapers, which took advantage of their special contacts with Russ-Photo and the labour photographers' associations. The well-known *Arbeiter Illustrierte Zeitung,* a German illustrated magazine published by the communist Willi Münzenberg, and the French illustrated magazine *Regards,* dedicated a cover to the celebrations each year.[26] More modest publications also came from mass organisations, such as *Facts about the Soviet Union,* the international newsletter of the Friends of the Soviet Union, the British section of which had the journal *Russia Today.*[27] The timing of articles in these publications around the commemorations responded to a relatively rigid organisation: a general issue on the USSR and its progress in the various fields prepared readers for the 7 November anniversary. The next issue then published pictures of the commemoration itself as it took place on the streets of Moscow.[28]

Radio broadcasting was also very well-suited to the international representation of the commemorations. Still on the fringes in the 1920s, radio, which gradually penetrated the media landscape of most of the European countries, enabled the Soviets to reach a much larger audience. The USSR, which had several transmitters from the early 1930s, broadcast commemorative transmissions abroad in German, English, French, Dutch, and Esperanto, and in later years also in Spanish and Chinese. Working-class amateur radio enthusiasts also circulated the celebrations on their networks. The October programme on the Moscow airwaves comprised: reading speeches by Soviet leaders, musical and theatrical broadcasts, and interviews with foreigners visiting the USSR for the commemorations. The numerous compositions in honour of October created by Shostakovitch, Prokofiev (*Symphony Number Five*), Khatchaturian, Mosolov, Glière, Nebolsin, Muradeli, Khrennikov and Myaskovsky were also available abroad in the form of records.

However, the most prominent field in which the international echo of the October commemorations benefited from the technological revolutions was in moving pictures: newsreels and, later, television. From the 1920s, newsreels enabled the Soviets to broadcast moving pictures with commentaries on the October commemorations, through exchange systems between large cinematographic groups (including Pathé).[29] The rise of fascism in Italy, Germany, Spain, and Portugal prevented almost all broadcasting about the USSR in those countries in the 1930s. But other countries, such as Britain and France, first of all sporadically and then regularly after the war, broadcast reports about 7 November.[30] Unlike the images broadcast in militant circles, the commemorative and celebratory discourse that the Soviets wished to convey was immediately hijacked. In western newsreels, the original Soviet images were cut up, put back together differently, and sometimes even erased. The propagandist content of the original discourse was sometimes left in, but commentaries were added that made fun of the spectacle or expressed the tensions between east and west. In these conditions, the initial celebration of the October events became a pretext for sizing up and, above all, denigrating one's opponents.

This dimension was further heightened for the television productions that accompanied the Cold War. In the 1950s with the arrival and then the general availability of TV receivers, broadcasts became one of the key components of the organisation of the celebrations as a spectacle.[31] Television gradually took on the status of prominent participant, making its mark on the event; the October celebrations had all the qualities of a television show. Theatrical illusions, backed up by a set of rites and symbols of the legitimacy of power, the programmes fitted in with the typology of 'media events' – or 'television ceremonies' or 'festive television' – as defined by Daniel Dayan and Elihu Katz.[32] Due to its universality, bringing together vast territories within the same moment in time, the television choreography of the October celebrations brought the spectator to the festival and made them a participant in it. While live broadcasting of the event made it possible to reach an even bigger audience, the impact of this ceremonial television still remained somewhat ambiguous. By broadcasting live, then in multiple recordings, the image of an ideal society embodied by the festival, Soviet TV appears to have taken up the baton of the agitprop, extending the field of propaganda to private spaces.[33] From this point of view, the viewers did not have complete freedom of choice. They were also encouraged to watch the event by inviting colleagues or neighbours round and by dressing up. However, watching the celebrations on TV in a private setting paradoxically rebuilt the barrier between players and spectators that the Communist celebrations were supposed to overcome. In this respect, it embodied to perfection the Brezhnev compromise between privatisation of the celebrations and superficial acceptance of their political ramifications by the population.

While the mass media contributed to the amplification of the spectacle of the celebrations, and to their international circulation, dissemination was not homogeneous. It covered different processes, the Soviet commemorative discourse in the satellite countries, but also its distortion by opponents. Television broadcasting first of all concerned the neighbouring countries. Like a number of the people's democracies, East German TV (*Deutscher Fernsehfunk*, DFF) and Hungarian TV broadcasted many Soviet programmes, including the October parade ritual. 'From eight o'clock in the morning, every 7 November', recalls Hungarian historian Kati Jutteau, 'we would sit in front of the television, because we were two hours behind them'.[34] But this televised ritual also affected the western democracies. Every year in the United States, regularly in Great Britain, France, and Italy and more exceptionally in Switzerland, the parade organised for the October commemorations was broadcast by the national broadcasters. In this context, it was not to obtain public support but, on the contrary, to suggest to viewers the dangers that might threaten them. The broadcasting of the military parade thus formed part of the staging of the Cold War. It fulfilled the same mobilising function as for the Soviet audience, but in the opposite direction.[35] The programme mobilised military experts and Sovietologists, or Kremlinologists.[36] The interest of the former was concentrated on the appearance of the troops and the presentation of the new arms (tanks, aircraft, missile launchers, and rockets). The latter used the broadcast to sketch out hypotheses about the balance of Soviet power, depending on the places occupied on the platform by the various leaders. Last-minute cancellation of the popular parade, as in 1974, aroused speculation about the state of health of one or other of the main leaders. In short, the broadcasting of the celebrations served as a pretext for a discussion about the state of the regime.[37]

THE EXTENSION OF THE TERRITORY OF THE CELEBRATIONS OUTSIDE SOVIET BORDERS

Commemorative events were also held outside the Soviet Union, constituting another aspect of the international reach of the October Revolution. Communist communities around the world also sought to celebrate a date that was understood as an integral part of their own triumphal revolutionary calendars. They appropriated the October Revolution to legitimate local projects as parts of a wider history of social and political achievements. Initially, they were small events, organised spontaneously – in Zurich in 1918, Turin 1919, Beijing 1923, but also in Prague, London, Paris, Chicago, etc – small street processions, lectures, discussions in factories, an evening at a community centre, evidence of the hopes the revolution inspired beyond its borders. But in 1927, mass meetings took place in Berlin,[38] Paris, London, New York, with workers' banquets and the projection of Soviet films.[39] An exhibition of fifteen pictures travelled across Europe and the Americas, under the title 'Ten years of socialist edification', putting the Soviet Union on international display.[40] Agitprop theatre troupes in the image of the famous Blue Shirts from the Moscow union toured the capitals of Europe in autumn 1927.[41] In many countries, workers organised strikes in solidarity with the Soviet working class.[42]

The internationalisation of the celebrations became progressively enmeshed in a highly structured context that included Soviet institutions (embassies, trade departments, and cultural missions), the Communist International, and the many mass organisations that orbited the Communist Parties – in the manner of, for example, the Friends of the Soviet Union. During the 1930s, the prohibition in most countries of communist parties and associations that were sympathetic to them gradually reduced the scale of the October commemorations. Only the Soviet embassies, where they existed, perpetuated the tradition, but discreetly and behind closed doors.

In 1939 and 1940, the October commemorations took part in the Sovietisation of the territories and peoples annexed by the Red Army following the Nazi-Soviet Pact.[43] Operation Barbarossa in 1941 marked a temporary constriction of the territory of the celebrations.

The military victories of the Soviet Union in the 'Great Patriotic War' led to broadening the field of the Soviet culture of commemoration. Initially, this took in the newly 'liberated' areas, with the 7 November celebrations taking place across a Russia that extended from Kaliningrad to Sakhalin, as well as in the Baltic countries and in Moldavia. Next, the people's democracies integrated the date of the October Revolution into their official calendar, and also reproduced the Soviet commemorative model with their own national days, albeit with efforts to mark them with certain national variations.[44]

In capitalist countries, the Soviets took advantage of the new prestige of the USSR, victor of the Second World War, in order to hold commemorative events. In Vienna, the philharmonic orchestra staged the opera *Boris Godunov* to celebrate the twenty-eighth anniversary of the revolution, which was watched by General Konev. In Berlin, Soviet soldiers used the thirtieth anniversary commemorations to place wreaths on the monument to the Russian dead in the British sector. In Washington, the Soviet ambassador, Vychinski, organised commemorative receptions over several years. These last manifestations of the great alliance against Nazism gradually disappeared with the advent of the Cold War.

The echo of October nonetheless persisted in western communist microsocieties in the form of meetings, concerts, and conferences. This was particularly the case in France and Italy, where the communist parties represented up to one quarter of the electorate in the 1950s and 1960s. On the fortieth anniversary of the revolution, the French Communist Party organised a large meeting in the hall of the *Mutualité*, with speeches by Soviet and French communist leaders, followed by a dance.[45]

The commemorative territory of October then developed in line with the many changes of regime that affected the Third World. Egypt, North Vietnam, and then Cuba opened the door to Soviet commemorative practices to prove their socialist allegiances. The former civic square of Havana, which had been transformed into Revolution Square, hosted the Cuban October marches.[46] Many of these new socialist countries, especially in Africa, often just marked the event by issuing a commemorative October stamp.[47]

Yet the celebrations also led to various forms of counter-demonstrations, commemorative demonstrations that attempted to give an alternative interpretation of the October Revolution. This was the case in the organisations and publications of the Mensheviks, the Trotskyites, and other radical left-wing movements. And there were counter-demonstrations aiming to denounce the Soviet regime that had resulted from the October Revolution. In 1967, the American anti-communists organised a counter-anniversary in Washington, to commemorate the victims of communism. In West Berlin, a Sovietologists conference was held to mark the occasion of the fiftieth anniversary. And finally, there was the *Biennale del Dissenso Culturale* (Biennial of Cultural Dissent),[48] organised in Venice in 1977 in reaction to the festivities planned by the Italian Communist Party and the Soviet embassy. The October celebrations were also the excuse for hijacking and hostile demonstrations.

CONCLUSION: A COMMEMORATIVE GEOGRAPHY OF OCTOBER

Overall, the international echo of the celebrations enables us to sketch out a map of the October territories, which means the part of the international space that was taken over by the supporters of the October Revolution. This is what we might call the 'territory of the comrades'. There were three types of these partisan territories: state spaces (the Soviet Union and its sister countries);[49] associative spaces (the party and the affiliated associations, that constituted communist micro-societies in some places, e.g. a town, sometimes a district, a factory, a community centre); and symbolic spaces (the colour of the comrades, red, indicating allegiance on the flags and banners; the October songs; the *Internationale;* and the comrades' commemorative calendar).

Despite its importance, October was merely one of many festivals in the Soviet calendar. During the Cold War, Soviet sympathisers, and particularly members of the communist parties, celebrated the key dates of the red calendar every year. There was the October Revolution, of course, but also the creation of the Soviet Union (on 30 December), Lenin's birthday (on 22 April), the First of May, Victory Day, and the leaders' birthdays.⁵⁰ But these partisan territories were not homogeneous. The chapters in this volume show all the unique echoes of October and their significance, in different countries and contexts. However, all chapters also emphasise the place of the celebrations in the same period of commemorative space and time. The celebrations contributed to the union of peoples and territories, both in the USSR and outside it.

Jean-François Fayet
January 2017

NOTES

1. Telegram from Trotsky to the CC of the PCR, 1920, RGASPI, f. 17, d. 60, l. 163, Moscow.
2. Polovtseva, the VOKS representative in England, 18 October 1927, GARF, f. 5283, op. 8, l. 47, Moscow.
3. Christopher Binns, 'The Changing Face of Power: Revolution and Accomodation in the Development of the Soviet Ceremonial System', Part I-II, *MAN* [*Journal of Royal Anthropological Institute*], Vol. 14 No. 4, December 1979, pp555-606 and Vol. 15 No. 1, March 1980, pp170-187; G. Gerodnik, 'Eto nado zhivym', *Prazdniki, obryady, traditsii,* Moskva, 1976; Vladimir V. Glebkin, *Ritual v sovetskoj kul'ture,* 'Ianus-K': Moskva, 1998; Emilia Koustova, 'Les fêtes révolutionnaires russes entre 1917 et 1920. Des pratiques multiples et une matrice commune', *Cahiers du monde russe,* Vol. 47 No. 4, 2006, pp683-714; Emilia Koustova, 'Célébrer, mobiliser et mettre en scène: le spectaculaire dans les manifestations festives soviétiques des années 1920', *Sociétés et Représentations,* Vol. 1 No. 31, 2011, pp157-176; Svetlana Malysheva, *Sovetskaya prazdnicnaya kul'tura v* provincii (1917-1927), Kazanskij Gosudarstvennyj Universitet: Kazan, 2005; Anatolii I. Mazaev, *Prazdnik kak sotsial'no-khudozhestvennoe iavlenie. Opyt istoriko-teoreticheskogo issledovaniia,* Izdatel'stvo 'Nauka': Moskva, 1978; Oleg V. Nemiro, *V gorod prishel prazdnik: Iz istorii khudozhestvennogo oformleniia sovetskikh massovykh prazdnestv,* Izdatel'stvo 'Avrora': Leningrad, 1973; Karen Petron, *Life Has Become More Joyous, Comrades: Celebrations in the Time of Stalin,* Indiana

University Press: Bloomington (IN), 2000; Malte Rolf, *Sovetskij massovyj prazdnik v Voroneže i Central'no-Černozemnoj Oblasti Rossii (1927-1932)*, Izdatel'stvo voronežskogo gosudarstvennogo Universiteta: Voronež, 2000; Malte Rolf, *Soviet Mass Festivals, 1917-1991*, Pittsburgh University Press: Pittsburgh, 2013 (2006).
4. Anatolij Vasil'eviã Lunatcharskij, *Ob iskusstve*, Iskusstvo: Moskva, 1982, p57.
5. Frederick C. Corney, *Telling October: memory and the making of the Bolshevik Revolution*, Cornell University Press: Ithaca, 2004.
6. Sophie Coeuré, *Pierre Pascal, La Russie entre christianisme et communisme*, Noir sur Blanc: Lausanne, 2014, p88.
7. Agitpropotdel du CC, RGASPI, f. 17, d. 60, l.7.
8. List of foreign delegates, RGASPI, f. 495, d. 99, l. 19, doc. 153, and GARF, f. 5283, op. 8, l. 47. Sophie Coeuré, 'Les "fêtes d'Octobre" à Moscou. La dynamique des structures d'influence soviétique et kominternienne autour d'un anniversaire', *Communisme*, No. 42-43-44, 1995, pp57-74.
9. Michael David-Fox, *Showcasing the Great Experiment: Cultural Diplomacy and Western Visitors to the Soviet Union, 1921-1941*, Oxford University Press: Oxford, 2012, pp127-141.
10. Susan M. Corbesero, 'The Anniversaries of the October Revolution, 1918-1927: Politics and Imagery', PhD, University of Pittsburgh, 2005, p185.
11. Bela Kun, secretary of ECCI, 30 November 1925, RGASPI, f. 495, d. 30, l. 141, doc.159 and f. 495, d. 60, l. 117, doc. 43-49.
12. International sub-commission, December 1926, RGASPI, f. 495, d. 60, l. 117.
13. Kurella, Agitpropotdel ECCI, to CC of the CPs, 4 February 1927, RGASPI, f. 496, d. 30, l. 376, doc. 8.
14. Münzenberg's proposition to the tenth anniversary of October Revolution, 14 November 1926, RGASPI, f. 495, d. 30, l. 264, doc. 132-135.
15. RGASPI, f. 495, d. 30, l. 392, doc. 51.
16. O. D. Kameneva, 11 February 1927, GARF, f. 5283, op. 1, l. 76, doc. 309.
17. Rachel Mazuy, *Croire plutôt que voir ? Voyages en Russie soviétique (1919-1939)*, Odile Jacob: Paris, 2002, pp99-102.
18. See for example: *Sowjet-Russland. Bericht der schweizerischen Arbeiter-Delegation, Oktober/November 1927*, Unionsdruckerei: Zürich, 1928.

19. Lists of foreign delegates (1928-1937), GARF, f. 5283, op. 8, ll. 111-330.
20. Lists of foreign delegates (1948-1957), GARF, f. 5283, op. 8, ll. 331-352.
21. N.G. Tomilina (Gl. red.), *Nasledniki Kominterna. Meždunarodnye sovesanija predstavitelej kommunističeskih i rabočih partij v Moskve (nojabr' 1957): Dokumenty*, Moskva: ROSSPÈN, 2013
22. RGASPI, M-1/30/1489, 1977.
23. Gianni Haver, Jean-François Fayet, Valérie Gorin, Emilia Koustova (eds), *Le spectacle de la révolution : La culture visuelle des commémorations d'Octobre, en URSS et ailleurs*, Antipodes: Lausanne, 2017.
24. The most famous was the German edition of the *Illustrierte Geschichte der russischen Revolution*, written under the direction of W. Astrow A. Slepkow and J. Thomas, for which the contract was signed in 1926 by Neuer Deutscher Verlag.
25. *Die Rote Fahne, L'Humanité, L'Unità* developed the theme: 'Why the October anniversary is our celebration too'.
26. Heinz Willmann, *Geschichte der Arbeiter Illustrierte Zeitung*, Verlag Das Europ. Buch: Berlin, 1974.
27. Jean-François Fayet, *VOKS. Le laboratoire helvétique. Histoire de la diplomatie culturelle soviétique durant l'entre-deux-guerres*, Georg: Genève, 2014, p414.
28. Gianni Haver 'La révolution recadrée. La presse illustrée de l'Europe occidentale pendant l'entre-deux-guerres', in Haver, Fayet, Gorin and Koustova, *op.cit.*, pp158-177.
29. Luke McKernan, *Yesterday's news: the British cinema newsreel reader*, British Universities Film & Video Council: New York, 2002.
30. Valérie Gorin et Gianni Haver, 'Les commémorations de la révolution russe d'octobre 1917 dans la presse filmée occidentale (1947-1967)', *Traverse*, No. 2, 2016, pp136-150.
31. Ellen Propper Micklewicz, *Split Signals: Television and Politics in the Soviet Union*, Oxford University Press: New York, 1988; Christine E. Evans, *Between Truth and Time: A History of Soviet Central Television*, Yale University Press: New Haven and London, 2016, p83.
32. Daniel Dayan et Elihu Katz, *La Télévision Cérémonielle*, PUF: Paris, 1996, p12; James Carey, 'Political ritual on television: episodes in the history of shame, degradation and excommunication', in James Curran and Tamar Liebes (eds), *Media, Ritual, Identity*, Routledge: London, 1998, pp42-70.

33. Kristian Feigelson, 'En URSS, la télévision a-t-elle pris la relève de l'Agit prop ?', in, Marc Ferro (dir.), *Film et histoire*, EHESS: Paris, 1984.
34. Kati Jutteau, *L'enfance embrigadée dans la Hongrie communiste. Le mouvement des pionniers*, L'Harmattan: Paris, 2007, p155.
35. Valérie Gorin, 'La commémoration cathodique. La retransmission télévisuelle des fêtes aux Etats-Unis', in Haver, Fayet, Gorin and Koustova, *op. cit.* pp253-258.
36. David C. Engerman, *Know Your Enemy: The Rise and Fall of America's Soviet Experts*, Oxford University Press: Oxford, 2009.
37. Whitman Bassow, *The Moscow correspondents. Reporting on Russia from the Revolution to Glasnost*, Paragon House: New York, 1989.
38. 'Demonstration in Berlin for the tenth anniversary', *Sovkino-zhurnal*, RGAKFD, No. 48/106, 1927.
39. *October* by Eisenstein, based on the book by John Reed (*Ten Days That Shook The World*), Pudovkin's *End of St. Petersburg* and Barnet's *Moscow in October*. Alexandre Sumpf, *Révolutions russes au cinéma. Naissance d'une nation: URSS, 1917-1985*, Armand Colin: Paris, 2015.
40. Soviet Exhibition, 'Ten years of socialist edification', RGASPI, f. 495, d. 30, l. 373, doc. 91-176.
41. Kasper Braskén, *The International Workers' Relief, Communism, and Transnational solidarity. Willi Münzenberg in Weimar Germany*, Palgrave: Basingstoke, 2015, pp178-180.
42. Report on Lithuania, 29 November 1927, RGASPI, f. 495, d. 30, l. 371, doc. 264.
43. Irina Tcherneva, 'La Révolution d'Octobre dans le film documentaire balte soviétique (1940-1968)', in Haver, Fayet, Gorin and Koustova, *op. cit.*, pp213-230.
44. Jürgen Danyel, 'Politische Rituale als Sowjetimport', in Konrad H. Jarausch & Hannes Siegrist (Hg.), *Amerikanisierung und Sowjetisierung in Deutschland 1945-1970*, Campus Verl. Cop.: Frankfurt/Main, 1997, pp67-88; Monika, Gibas, 'Die Inszenierung kollektiver Identität. Staatssymbolik und Staatsfeiertage in der DDR', *Universitas. Zeitschrift für interdisziplinäre Wissenschaft*, No. 4, 1999, pp312-325.
45. www.cinearchives.org/Catalogue-d-exploitation-MARCEL-CACHIN-DOCUMENTS-494-1063-0-1.html?ref=5a728727717b789d667feea90aadd844, 28 July 2017.

46. Pablo Alonso González, 'The organization of Commemorative space in postcolonial Cuba: From Civic Square to Square of the Revolution', *Organization,* Vol. 23 No. 1, 2016, p56.
47. *Sovetskij sojuz na inostrannykh markakh,* Sviaz: Moskva, 1979.
48. Matteo Bertelé and Sandra Frimmel (eds), *La nuova arte sovietica: una prospettiva non ufficiale/ZKK Rereading: Die Dissens-Biennale 1977 in Venedig,* Edition Schublade: Zürich, 2014.
49. The different phases of the commemorations related to the Soviet Union allow us to shape a general overview of the official relations between these countries and Moscow.
50. Kevin Morgan, *International Communism and the Cult of the Individual. Leaders, Tribunes and Martyrs under Lenin and Stalin,* Palgrave: Basingstoke, 2017.

Commemorating an Event That Never Occurred: Russia's October in Soviet Ukraine in the 1920s

Eric Aunoble[1]

In Ukraine, the Bolsheviks faced a real challenge in promoting the October Revolution in the 1920s. As the editors of *Letopis Revolyutsii (The Chronicle of Revolution: The Ukrainian journal of Revolution and Communist Party History Studies)* wrote in its first issue in 1922: 'There was no October in Ukraine in the real meaning of the word'.[2] In fact, the only events that occurred in October-November 1917 were a failed red insurrection in Kiev (11-13 November, or 29-31 October, old calendar) and then the proclamation of the Ukrainian People's Republic by the moderate left-wing nationalists of the Central Rada on 7 (20) November.

This relative quietness is not surprising. The October Revolution consisted less of the spectacular occupation of various public buildings than of a general process of rank-and-file empowerment in factories, villages and regiments, which did also take place in Ukraine. It was not only Ukraine that seemed calm, but every region in the former Russian empire except for the two capital cities, Petrograd and Moscow, where Bolshevik uprisings did take place.

But Ukraine was no ordinary region. A national movement was trying to raise high the new yellow and blue flag and to advocate autonomy, if not at first independence. As a consequence, the problems of Ukraine resonated far more widely than those of other places. Even though the Bolsheviks were leading workers' protests in Ukraine's east and south-east (Donbass), their legitimacy in the region remained weak. Not all the Soviets had supported their October coup d'état, even in the east. In the all-Russian elections for the Constituent Assembly on 12 (25) November, while overall Lenin's party gained an average of 24 per cent of the vote, in Ukraine only 10 per cent of voters took their side. This shed light on the pressing need for the Bolsheviks to legitimate their power once the civil war ended in 1921.

They could not avoid using October, as it was the central motif in the new power's mythology throughout the Soviet Union. However, on the other hand, they also had to carefully consider how to make this a date both politically and nationally appropriate for Ukrainians, and how to make it a popular Ukrainian holiday. On the basis of the Ukrainian Soviet press and archival materials of the central committee of the Communist Party of Ukraine, we will trace here the evolution of this phenomenon, focusing on those years when the preparation of the October holiday generated the most documents: 1921, 1922 and 1927.

OCTOBER IN THE UKRAINIAN SOVIET PANTHEON

The ending of the civil war clearly had an impact on the way that official holidays were celebrated. As an internal memorandum for the preparation of the first of May celebrations in 1921 says: 'The hard armed struggle left an indelible imprint on the character of proletarian holidays, but [now] the joyful force of toiling masses is beating its way out from under the armour of wartime'.[3] Indeed, looking at the official Soviet calendar, holidays appear to have flourished at the beginning of the 1920s and one may be surprised to discover that October is only one holiday among many others. Using almanacs and other contemporary sources, a chronological list of anniversaries and other occasions is: in January, Bloody Sunday (9 January 1905); in February, the foundation of the party (27 February 1898); in March, the abolition of serfdom (4 March 1861), the foundation of the Third International (4 March 1919), International Working Women's Day (8 March), the February revolution (12 March 1917) and the Paris Commune (18 March 1871); in April, the Lena massacre (17 April 1912); in May, International Workers' Day (1 May) and the foundation of *Pravda* (5 May 1912). In the second half of the year, there is then only 'Youth Day' (6 September) and the 'Day of the Proletarian Revolution' (7 November) as dates to be feted.[4]

The significance of political holidays: usefulness vs meaning

As one might guess, if only from the accumulation of dates in March, not all the holidays were celebrated equally. Except for 1 May and 7 November, most were only an opportunity for political education through a lecture or an exhibition. Even so, jubilees could be emphasised, as for example those of the Paris Commune in 1921 (fiftieth anniversary), the foundation of *Pravda* in 1922 (tenth anniversary), or the party's foundation in 1923 (twenty-fifth anniversary).[5] The October Revolution itself was particularly feted on the fifth and tenth anniversaries in 1922 and 1927. To this extent, institutions could therefore make their choice of what to emphasise between the different events.

All of the dates were linked with memorials, and this was also true of the first of May. This was still something quite novel for people in the Soviet Union, and was linked to illegal meetings such as the first 'Mayovka' in Kharkov in 1900. Nevertheless, the guidance given by the Communist Party's central committee section for agitation and propaganda went a long way beyond purely historical concerns. In the various internal memoranda that it issued, each holiday was seen to be legitimised by a political agenda considered in an educational way. On 9 January 1905:

> Unconscious and uncontrolled [*stixijnye*] St. Petersburg workers went out in the street with faith in God and the Tsar, under the leadership of an adventurer and provocateur, priest Gapon ... the task of mourning speeches and meetings on this day [of commemoration] is to illuminate the long road towards eradicating illusions and to take the same path in memory again. Even now the tenacious remnants of these illusions persist in backward layers of the workers and peasant masses, the remnants of religious belief, of political consciousness, in the form of anarchism, Menshevism and syndicalism, which still burden the consciousness of those workers who are not members of the communist party.

Apart from the 'assessment of historical significance of the revolution of 1905', the aim of the holiday was thus to 'struggle against the remnants of religious faith' and to 'fight against political illusions, especially against Menshevism, and to evaluate rightly the harm brought to the proletariat by these illusions'.[6]

Regarding the Lena massacre, agitators were to explain how the workers' movement had acted at that time, highlighting the role played by the party and its newspaper *Pravda*, and to emphasise the improvement of labour legislation since 1912. The February revolution was to be depicted 'as a prologue for October' and 'the role of the Party within it' was to be clearly insisted upon. Similarly, the 'content of the agitation and propaganda on 18 March, day of memory, is to explain the Paris Commune as the first experience of proletarian dictatorship, to consider [the importance] of this experience and its failures, to oppose them with the achievements of the proletarian revolution in Russia'.[7]

Essentially, this saw the fiftieth anniversary of the Commune as a way of popularising support for the Red Army.

The October anniversaries were thought of in the same utilitarian way. For 1921, the first slogan was 'in the fourth year of the October Revolution, no proletarian in any party except the communist party'. As the countryside was starving, another motto proclaimed 'October is a struggle against hunger and cold: collect grain, chop wood'.[8] Clearly, historical events were interpreted from a present-day perspective. The same approach also prevailed at an all-union level. Thus, the manifesto issued for 1922 by the central section for agitation and propaganda in Moscow was focused on the international and internal 'situation of the Soviet republic' and barely mentioned what had happened five years earlier.[9]

As the directions for these revolutionary jubilees appeared to combine a liturgical calendar with useful hints and suggestions for the day, one can understand why there was not much place for a potential local aspect. A certain date had to be commemorated as a part of a global scansion of time and as a means to promote current priorities: the fact that one was located in Moscow, Kharkiv, or Chukotka did not have not much importance. Ukraine merited a place in this discursive system only as an element of context. For instance, manifestos for the 1921 festival stated:

> After a long period of Civil War, which had Ukraine for its arena ... we have a break and we can switch to peaceful building work.

> The revolution is not a sudden jump into the joyful kingdom of toilers. It is the beginning of a years-long worldwide revolution ... This understanding demands a deep approach to assess this four-year period before the masses ... In Ukraine, this

four-year development of the revolution took place in a very particular situation [*svoeobraznaja obstanovka*]. The meaning of each moment of struggle was constantly covered by the upcoming events. The task of Party propaganda during the October festival week is to restore these events in their strict continuity and in their historical richness of meaning.[10]

So, in order to fulfil this claim, we will look at the historical discourse in which the October Revolution was explained to the Ukrainian masses and see how the events were organised.

COMMEMORATION AS A WAY TO DEFINE A HISTORICAL OBJECT: AN IDEOLOGICAL AND CHRONOLOGICAL FRAME FOR OCTOBER

The second of these quotations indicates that 'revolution' is to be understood in an extended way, as a 'four-year period of revolution in Ukraine'. In this long process, beginning with the overthrow of tsarism and ending with the civil war, the events of October were indeed only an episode, the importance of which was not factual but rather symbolic and ideological. The issue was not therefore whether something occurred in Ukraine on 25 October or not, but which side you had taken in those years. The meaning of the whole phenomenon was rooted in the social and political realities of the time: on one side stood the Bolsheviks and the proletariat, while on the other side one would find the reactionary parties and classes.

The division between friends and enemies was based on Marxism, but it also relied on wider cultural references. These are very evident in the 'List of theatre plays recommended by the Scientific council for repertoire ... for staging on the day of the fifth anniversary of the October revolution'.[11] These seventy-five plays deserve study in their own right, but for the present time it is sufficient to notice that they portray the entire history of humanity's movement for emancipation. For example, the list included *Spartacus* by Vladimir Volkenstein, *The Jacquerie* by Prosper Mérimée, set in the middle ages, *The Death of Copernicus* by A. Terek (Olga Forsh's pseudonym), and four plays about the Paris Commune by the Russian-Soviet authors Borisov, Galin, Lvov and Arsky. There were also four plays devoted to the French Revolution of the eighteenth century.[12] Along with the left-wing playwrights Romain Rolland (*The Storming of the Bastille*) and Andrey Globa (*The Day Marat Died*), it is surprising to find among the plays somewhat reactionary authors like Paul Bourget (*Christmas Night During the Terror*, adapted by Sarah Bernhardt's husband Maurice)[13] and Paul Claudel (*The Hostage*). The fact that Claudel's play was renamed *The Avenger* leads one to imagine that the ideological content of the play was inverted: the cruelty of the revolutionaries was to be seen as a virtue.

Framing the October Revolution within such a long-term narrative allows us to understand why the particularities of Ukraine might seem an accessory to the wider commemorations, as a detail that could be either included or disregarded in a presentation. For instance, a curriculum of political literacy for technical and professional schools in 1921 totally ignored Ukraine and dealt with the revolution as a whole, from the point of view of the empire's capital cities, Petrograd and Moscow.[14] This curriculum was copied from a textbook edited in Soviet Russia and was used nevertheless in Kharkov, the new capital city of Soviet Ukraine. One should not necessarily see in this a malicious attempt to erase everything Ukrainian. Kharkov's population was overwhelmingly not Ukrainian, but Russian and Jewish, as in most Soviet Ukrainian towns.[15]

Similarly, many Bolshevik cadres were not locals, as they had arrived in Ukraine after drifting along the powerful streams of the civil war since 1918.[16] Their situation as professional revolutionaries with no place they could identify as 'home' did not help to root their discourse in Ukrainian soil. Neither did their ideology help. The 1922 *Theses for the celebration of the fifth anniversary of the October Revolution* offers an interesting insight into the significance of national factors for Ukrainian Bolsheviks:

> The Russian [*rossijskij*] proletariat appears as a part of the world proletariat. The victory of the Russian proletariat is possible only [by achieving] union with the workers of all countries. The anniversary of the October Revolution appears to be an international holiday, a day of international solidarity. For the fifth anniversary of the October Revolution, the proletariat of the Soviet republics will welcome the representatives of proletarian parties coming to Petrograd for the fourth congress of the Communist International.[17]

The choice of words is rather interesting. 'Rossijskij' clearly refers not to a nationality as a cultural entity, but to the sense of belonging to the former Russian empire, and hence the 'rossijskij proletariat' is that now organised in various 'Soviet republics', including the Ukrainian one. But fundamentally, these matters were not considered very important, for it was the international essence of the exploited class that was brought to the fore.

The issue was not only whether or not to talk about Ukraine, but also how to talk about it. In *Five Years of Revolution in Ukraine 1917-1921*, which was planned for publication in 1922,[18] analysis did not rely on a national scheme at all. The 'National Question' was the focus of only one of the fourteen chapters. Specifically Ukrainian topics (such as the *Rada* and the Autocephalous Church) represented only a fifth of the project. What appears to us as the Ukrainian specificity of those years, its national movement, was only marginal to the volume as planned. Local political parties appear, for instance, to have been of no more importance than all-Russian Mensheviks or social-revolutionaries (SRs). We should exercise caution here, for there is more than a grain of truth in this. The national movement became historically important retrospectively, as Ukraine finally gained its independence after 1991. In marked contrast, for the nationalist supporters of the early 1920s, the fate of their purely 'Ukrainian revolution' between 1917 and 1921 appeared to be a complete failure. One could hardly expect a more positive point of view on nationalism from the winners in this contest, the Bolsheviks!

No more surprising is the emphasis that the Bolsheviks put on the role of their own party. At this point, the utilitarian approach we outlined earlier became combined with a general conception of the revolution, in which the mass mobilisation of the poorest layers of the population eventually gave birth to a new society only thanks to the leadership of the Communist Party. While this Leninist stance is not surprising, the absence of reference to the economic and social basis for revolution is more unexpected. Revolution was clearly shown as the result of a struggle for power and not as an abstract historical necessity. But if, on the one hand, the Communist Party was depicted as the creator of history, on the other hand there was praise for the first achievements of Soviet Ukrainian socialism, which represented more than half of the planned book. This justified the whole path the country had followed since 1917 and was portrayed as the best reason to keep moving forward.

This tendency appears in various documents of the period. As early as 1921, the Communist Party's women's section (*zhenotdel*) magazine *Kommunarka Ukrainy* entitled its opening article 'Assessments'. Although it recognised the appalling state of the country after the civil war ended, it saw in the survival of Soviet power a decisive achievement which opened 'the way to communism ... through two steps. The first step – the victory against internal and external counter-revolution – is already completed

... The second step is to develop the productive forces in agriculture and industry'.[19] The following year, in 1922, an exhibition for the revolution's fifth anniversary was to 'illustrate the revolutionary development in Ukraine and also the five-year experience of social construction by workers under the leadership of the communist party'.[20] In the same fashion, a book to be issued by the women's section under the title of *Daughters of October* was divided into the following chapters: '1) An overview of the last five years. 2) Working class and peasant women on the war front. 3) Working class and peasant women on the work front.'[21]

It would be provocative to speak of 'permanent revolution', but nevertheless the events of 1917 or even of 1917-1921 were in this way dissolved into a process which was still ongoing. The efforts to set up a powerful Soviet economy were assimilated into the hardship of revolutionary struggle in a way which would bear rich dividends until the very end of the Soviet system.

COMMEMORATION AS ACTION

From the point of view of the central committee archives, the October commemorations were made up not so much of discourses but of action. Various state and party institutions were busy planning *meropriyatiya* [arrangements] for what was to be done and by whom. From 1921, special commissions were set up to organise and implement the commemorations. The initiative lay in the hands of the Communist Party, more precisely in its section for agitation and propaganda. At a provincial level, the section asked for representatives from the trade unions and from the political leadership of the Red Army.[22]

This was the usual architecture for political-educational work in the 1920s and it was finally headed by the *Politprosvet,* the state institution dealing with mass campaigning.[23] This implied that the mobilisation of material and human resources should rely essentially on the Communist Party, the army, and the unions. The army organised street demonstrations, while the unions provided their clubs near the working places and the working-class areas.[24] For wider gatherings, state-controlled theatres were necessary, and the party sent speakers to all of these events.[25]

The Istpart, a new institution to take control of the past

Although the activities of these commissions is worth studying, they represented only a temporary merging of pre-existing institutions. One of these was specifically linked with the commemorative process, namely the *Istpart*. This Commission for the History of the October Revolution and of the Communist Party was a permanent one. In Soviet Russia, it was founded in September 1920 as a state institution, and was transferred to central committee control in late 1921. In Ukraine, it was created in early 1922 directly as a party organation.[26] It did not really become active until the spring of that year, though even then it still had organisational problems.[27]

The first issue of its journal, *Letopis Revolyutsii* (*The Chronicle of Revolution*), was published 'For the fifth anniversary of the October Revolution', as it stated on the cover. Although the editorial stated that 'There was no October in Ukraine in the real meaning of the word',[28] the issue featured eighteen articles about the revolutionary events of 1917 in various places in Ukraine, Kharkov, Kiev, Donbass, Ekaterinoslav, Elizavetgrad, Nikolaev, Chernigov, and not forgetting the war front. Among the authors, who included leading Ukrainian Bolsheviks such as Grigory Petrovsky, Emanuel Kviring, Sylvestr Pokko, and Yan Ryappo, you could also find Moysey Ravich-Cherkassky, who was one of the leaders of *Istpart* and the chief editor of *Letopis Revolyutsii*. By this means, the seasoned activist, who was fighting against autocracy already in 1905, confirmed his movement towards becoming a historian: he had already published about Makhno's movement in 1920, and in 1923 was to become the first historian of the Communist Party of Ukraine.[29] For Mikhail Rubach the commemoration and the *Istpart* would also be the path to a career as a historian. Planning the 1921 October commemoration in the Ekaterinoslav province as head of the Communist Party's section for agitation and propaganda, he would contribute to *Letopis Revolyutsii* (1924), be in charge of archives (1927), and then become the head of the Ukrainian *Istpart* in 1929.[30]

From its founding in 1922, the first task of the central *Istpart* was to set up an all-Ukrainian network to organise archival material and assume control of it. Lacking sufficient financial resources, the *Istpart* quickly seemed to have reached an impasse, as it had to ask the central executive committee – i.e. the state – to fund archival repositories as soon as it had taken control over them.[31] Professional archivists from the *Tsentrarkhiv* resisted the hegemony of the *Istpart*, resulting in bureaucratic conflicts between the two institutions. The problem was finally solved in 1925, when the *Tsentrarkhiv* became responsible for pre-revolutionary material and *Istpart* for the documents dating from after 1917. Nevertheless, inspired by the Soviet diarchy between *spetsy* (bourgeois specialists) and red commissars, it was stipulated that *Istpart* would control the political use of all material, while *Tsentrarkhiv* would be responsible for the conservation of revolutionary and post-revolutionary documents.[32]

The need to keep a grip on the documents of the revolution had two aspects to it. On the one hand, the Communist Party acted as a controlling body, fearing that every leak could be used against its policy. In 1921, it asked the 'bourgeois' historian Dmitri Bagaley to write an article for a commemorative book.[33] Soon, however, only party members were authorised to investigate the archives, while the *Istpart* was in touch with the GPU (political police) about the documents' circulation.[34] At the same time, the *Istpart* developed a real historiographical effort to collect and utilise these materials. Local party branches and individual activists were firmly requested to send to the central *Istpart* documents of 'all-Ukrainian character' for the fifth anniversary.[35] The Istpart also collected documents issued by the former state apparatus (from governors, police and gendarmerie) 'although they [were] largely not objective'.[36]

These documents were mainly used to prepare commemorative exhibitions and collections of documents to be published for the anniversaries. Activists also wrote articles of either a purely memorial or wider historical character, but they were often late with their papers, just as they were reluctant to send their own documents.[37] In talking about the exhibition and publication of such materials, we have already moved from the institutional organisation of the commemoration to the action implemented by the institutions.

What is to be done

Publishing was indeed one of the main ways to celebrate October, as we saw with the first issue of *Letopis Revolyutsii* and the book *Five Years of Revolution in Ukraine 1917-1921*. These rather highbrow publications had real importance for authors. As mentioned above, leading Bolsheviks participated in the launching of *Letopis Revolyutsii*, and a special issue of *Kommunisticheskaya Mysl'* (*The Communist Idea*) involved two veterans of revolutionary battles, Dmitri Zatonsky and Vitaly Primakov, among other party officials.[38] The list of contributors to *Five Years* was even more impressive. Leading historians and intellectuals such as Ivanov (*Istpart*), Ryappo, Ravich-Cherkassky, and Yavorsky played their part, but the history was mainly told by renowned participants in the civil war such as Zatonsky (again), Stanislav Kossior, Mykola Skrypnyk and Vasyl Blakytny, the 'national communist'.[39] It was the head of the Ukrainian council of people's commissars, Christian Rakovsky himself, meanwhile, who wrote about the international situation of Soviet Ukraine. For those who doubt the political and institutional significance of it bearing such a signature, it is sufficient to say that the chapter about women was written by Filatova, the head of the women's section within the central committee.[40] Having one's name in the list of contributors to such a book indicated a high status within the organisational hierarchy of the Soviet apparatus.

We have no information about the actual audience for these journals and books. We only know that producing them for the October commemorations was considered a key priority. In 1921, for instance, the central committee's section for agitation and propaganda asked the *Kommunist,* the party daily newspaper, to print an extra 2000 copies to send to all provinces on 7 November.[41] Given that 2000 copies is not a significant number for a country of 25 million people, we still do not know anything about the actual readership of these materials. This gives the impression that commemoration priorities were somewhat self-referential.

This hypothesis can be verified by checking some of the celebration plans prepared by various commissions for the organisation of the October Revolution's anniversary. The template was well-established and the same arrangements are to be found in a local project for Ekaterinoslav in 1921 as in an all-Ukrainian circular for 1922. Members of the Communist Party and trade unions were summoned to an organisational meeting before the holiday. Institutions for children such as schools and orphanages were also required to prepare their own celebrations. On the day itself, street parades would be a joint enterprise of the Red Army, the party, and the trade unions. However, 'the Red Army parade, as a demonstration of its readiness to fight, should not obscure the popular character of the celebration; it should emphasise its unity with the masses of workers and peasants' (1922). A solemn session of the local Soviet would complete the agenda, and in the evening theatres and clubs would offer free shows with singing and acting, but only on revolutionary themes.[42]

Is a working class hero something to be?

Another interesting point in the commemorative plans is the place allocated to the main forces of the revolution: workers and activists. The way workers' activism during the revolution was emphasised is rather paradoxical. For instance, the Ekaterinoslav commission for the October commemoration encouraged the organisation of 'memorial evenings' (*večer pamjati*) on 6 November 1921. The 'memorial evenings' bore close resemblance to the 'evenings of memories' (*večer vospominanij*) which were organised by the *Istpart* to collect testimonies by gathering together people to collectively recall what they had done for the party.[43] Political control over these evenings was visible in the selection of speakers by the local party committees or by the trade unions. They were organised as private events, open only to those who had received an invitation, whether communists or non-party members. They were meant to have a 'purely family character'.[44]

The impression created is that the living memory of revolutionary events was not intended to be transferred to the public sphere. Instead, the press preferred to talk about 'Martyrs and Heroes', as *Kommunarka Ukrainy,* the Communist Party's women's periodical, did in its 1921 commemorative special issue.[45] This described women who died for Soviet power, from the most famous to the previously anonymous. First, there were biographies of Ines Armand, Lenin's close friend, and Konkordia Samoilova, a Bolshevik woman who was active in Ukraine before the war and the founder of *Rabotnitsa*, the first communist women's magazine in Russia. After them followed the portraits of six Ukrainian peasant women who died during the civil war fighting against 'bandits', i.e. rural insurgents.

The only physical appearance of participants in the revolution was achieved through the valorisation of heroes. At the solemn session of the Soviet planned in Ekaterinoslav a 'march of the heroes of the army and the revolution' was scheduled, following which they were to receive as prizes 'books, banners and equipment'. In memorial evenings, the audience was a selected one, and consequently all were treated as equal, in dignity if not in status. With heroes, the case was quite different, as they were shown to the public and rewarded. They were also clearly separated from the masses by this display, and it is interesting to note what actions led to someone being defined as a 'hero': revolution, army, activism, and work. From 1921, the expression 'hero of labour' was commonplace and induced a confusion between high personal productivity and revolutionary heroism. For instance, an account of the 1922 commemoration in one of the districts of Kharkov states 'For some days, memorial evenings were organised at workplaces, honouring veterans of labour at the same time'.[46]

The study of the October commemorations helps us understand how a number of features of the fully developed Soviet system were born. The radical separation between a mass of admirers and an elite of heroes and leaders could be seen as a mechanical effect of the strengthening of a new bureaucratic power. Some documents shed a different light on this phenomenon, however, such as a 'Scheme for mass demonstrative action for the day of the fifth anniversary of the October Revolution in Kharkov'. 'Union processions' and 'processions through workplaces' with a 'theatricalised element' were planned. In one plant, artists, disguised as 'pre-revolutionary policemen' would disrupt workers' meetings; in another, artists would act as former bosses and capitalists and judge the misbehaviour of workers with the help of representatives of the 'foreign community'. In other factories, plays about bureaucratism and bribery, quizzes with prizes, or choral singing were to take place. These were meant to create a 'festive mood' among workers, so that the masses would 'receive from the artistic awakeners all the significance and the ideological content of the holiday'. Processions from all these various workplaces would then gather, and 'the masses who had been previously trained' would meet actors disguised as leaders (including Lenin) and rebuff a group of masked figures representing starvation and disease.[47]

This document is not inspired by some cold-blooded and short-sighted bureaucratism. On the contrary, it expresses real enthusiasm and a solid theoretical ground, both in politics and aesthetics. The production of collectivist art was the aim of this project, based on the artistic unity and consistency of the celebration.[48] This ambitious programme of *Gesamtkunstwerk*, mixing philosophical-religious vocabulary with political goals, was typical of the Proletkult (proletarian culture) movement. Although in Soviet Russia this movement was in 1920 almost abolished by forced integration in the *Narkompros* (the Commissariat for Enlightenment), it was formally founded in Ukraine only in late 1922 by communists who already worked at the Narkompros as officials.[49]

One of the key elements of the movement was the emphasis on the 'creative autonomy of the masses' [*tvorčeskaja samodejatel'nost' mass*]. However, this does not seem well-founded either from an artistic or a political point of view. The actions planned for the October commemorations were to be implemented by 'theatrical circles at [workers'] clubs and studios under the leadership of professional artists and stage directors'.[50] Fundamentally, the workers were considered as an inert material that would be impressed and shaped by those who knew how to master collective psychology, aesthetics, and revolutionary politics. Although this grandiose project might not have been fulfilled – it seems that Proletkult eventually organised its own celebration in a very traditional way with poetry readings and speeches[51] – it shows that the radical Proletkult activists, just like party potentates, took for granted the fact that the working class was essentially passive and should be taught how to celebrate its own revolution by the exhibition of leaders and heroes.

1927, A STRAINED COMMEMORATION

The year 1927, about which we have ample documentary evidence, was a crucial one, not only for Ukraine but for the whole Soviet Union. The symbolic tenth anniversary of October was the backdrop to the last political struggle before Stalin took over complete control of the party and state apparatuses by vanquishing the 'United opposition'. The public anti-Stalinist demonstrations at the October commemorations in November ended in defeat. A month later, the fifteenth party congress decided to 'cleanse the party of all clearly incorrigible elements of the Trotskyist opposition'.[52] Meanwhile, history and its representations remained a major issue: *October*, the film made for the occasion by Sergei Eisenstein, shed little light on Trotsky's role, and where it was informative, it was only negatively so.

The systematisation of memorial policing

From the point of view of Soviet Ukrainian periodicals, this background of political and ideological struggle seems as if it was completely absent, or at least separated, from the memorial concerns. Quite the contrary, the systematisation of all the processes for 1921-2 is striking, as highlighted. The central committee's section for agitation and propaganda was no longer obliged to send typewritten circulars to local party committees, for it now published its own periodical, *Agitatsia i propaganda*. In the October issue, there was an article explaining once and for all 'The historical significance of the October Revolution'. It insisted on international issues and internal economic ones, emphasising the priorities of Soviet power in 1927. The November issue printed forty-six ready-to-use slogans with the same purpose. In addition, *Kultrabotnik,* the organ of the trade unions' cultural section, proposed a complete survey of the preparation of the commemoration in various places and types of industry.[53]

With historiographical focus, both *Kultrabotnik* and *Letopys revolyutsii* offered their readers select bibliographies.[54] The selections were in both cases made in the same spirit of political rectitude, but they nevertheless reveal important differences. The trade union periodical presented works on the Russian revolution more generally, i.e. about the revolution in Russia, and it classified books by how difficult they were ('popular' / 'medium difficulty' / 'for well-versed readers'). The *Istpart* journal, in contrast, chose only books about the events in Ukraine and compared the strengths and weaknesses of various texts, all of the authors party leaders, many of whom had written on these themes for the fifth anniversary. It also provided nearly thirty articles in three sections: the revolution in various towns and regions, the role of the union movement, and to the memory of those who had died. This special issue reflected the organisational improvement of the work of the *Istpart.* It was now supervising a network of nineteen groups of veterans, comprising 500 people. It collected personal memories and accounts from memorial evenings, organised conferences and seminars, and provided material, not only for the journal, but also for exhibitions.[55]

These journals aimed at activists could not reach many people. The most successful exhibition might have 10,000 visitors, which again is not many in a country of 25 million people.[56] More popular periodicals did dedicate an issue to the October anniversary, but the event had virtually become a cliché of revolutionary heroism. The commemoration was just one more way of popularising the regime's obsessions: to demonstrate its achievements since 1917 and, especially in 1927, to denounce the attitude of the capitalist aggressors surrounding the first socialist state.[57]

We could find only one attempt to accommodate a developed historical narrative of these events intended for a larger audience. The weekly *Vsesvit*, a stronghold of the so-called 'national communists', presented its special issue with a cover showing the first *sovnarkom* (Council of People's Commissars) where Trotsky's portrait was directly to the left of Lenin's.[58] Inside, the issue covered all the revolutionary years from 1917 until the end of the civil war, in Russia and Ukraine, and both in the towns and in the countryside. Among the rich illustrative material, there were even photographs of nationalist leaders with the logotype of the Ukrainian People's Republic. Quite modern in its presentation, and not too narrowly focused either historically or ideologically, the example of *Vsesvit*'s special issue is a rare one.

But the issue was also remarkable in its willingness to discuss the Ukrainian aspect of the revolution along with the all-Russian narrative. We have seen how Ukrainian issues were almost absent in 1921-2. Four or five years after the revolution, the Bolsheviks' discourse was mainly self-referential, as if there were no need to justify October in any other terms that those of Marxism-Leninism. It was implied that the revolution was essentially the same wherever it happened, and it was therefore unnecessary to focus on local specificities. Only those Bolsheviks who had a special biographical link with Ukraine emphasised this aspect, but seemingly as a means to justify their own importance: as for example Skrypnyk (Lenin's Ukrainian), or the former leftist nationalist Blakytny. Although the latter did participate in the *Istpart* initiatives and had the opportunity to express their views publicly, their absence from the internal material issued by the central committee of the Communist Party of Ukraine regarding the October commemorations is striking. It is as if the organisational grafting of the Ukrainian revolutionary bough onto the

Bolshevik tree had had no influence, not only externally, but even on its inner system of ideological exposition.

A UKRAINIAN SUBSTITUTE FOR OCTOBER?

Some of the documentary evidence relating to 1927 leads us to believe that certain changes were afoot. Still, there was no relevant event that might have taken place in Ukraine in October/November 1917, and so there was a need to valorise what happened locally as a consequence of October more broadly. The insurrections in the Kiev Arsenal factory had been genuine workers' uprisings and were therefore quite suitable for this purpose. The first one had started five days after the Petrograd coup d'état, on 29 October (12 November) 1917, and had been celebrated on the fifth anniversary when the press announced the erection of a monument that was realised a few months later.[59] This was a decision of the city Soviet and was one of the attempts of Kievian communists to defend the revolutionary honour of their city, usually surpassed by Kharkov or Donbass.[60] Nevertheless, what was actually a real Ukrainian October did not become a national memorial event.

Conversely, the insurrection of January 1918 did become a symbol. Here, workers were opposed to the nationalist-orientated Central Rada, with fierce fighting and damage to the factory building where the fighting took place. When, in the following month Bolsheviks took over Kiev, they immediately reburied the 750 victims in a mass grave. In 1927, a monument was erected of which only a commemorative plaque now survives. The inscription on the bas-relief reads: 'Eternal remembrance for the freedom fighters – 10 October 1917-1927'. It thus explicitly commemorates October 1917 and not January 1918. This superimposition of the Russian October onto the Ukrainian January seems present in other spheres. The idea of a film on this subject was already present in 1927, as a counterpart to Eisenstein's project.[61]

It was eventually completed by Alexander Dovzhenko, the only Ukrainian filmmaker of the same stature.[62]

On reading the central committee's documents for 1927, it is apparent that the promotion of the January 1918 uprising at this time was not viewed as the main way of rooting Bolshevik history in Ukrainian soil. What most interested party leaders was the creation of a new memorial date commemorating the 'ten years of existence of Soviet power in Ukraine'. A special commission was set up and held its first meeting on 14 December 1927 with members of the all-Ukrainian executive committee, representatives of the People's Commissariats of Justice and Internal Affairs, the Kharkov regional party committee, the main Ukrainian newspaper (*Visti*), and the archives. Their first decision was to 'acknowledge the date of 25 December 1927, marking ten years since the beginning of Soviet power in Ukraine'. Then they planned this new commemoration on the very model that had been developed for the celebration of October.[63]

The date that was chosen corresponded to the proclamation of the Ukrainian Soviet republic by the all-Ukrainian congress of the Soviets. As the moderate Central Rada had proclaimed the Ukrainian People's Republic in late November, Lenin's *sovnarkom* issued an ultimatum against the Kiev authorities at the very beginning of December.[64] Consequently, Kharkov's congress of the Soviets might have appeared only as an episode in an impending Russian-Ukrainian war. For instance, the new Ukrainian historiography following independence in the 1990s immediately denied its 'all-Ukrainian' character, calling it the 'Donets and Krivoy Rog Basin's congress of soviets'.[65] However, it did anchor Ukrainian Soviet power in the country's far east, in Russian-speaking regions, close to Russia.

The date of 25 December 1917 in Kharkov is neither politically symbolic nor heroic, in contrast to 7 November in Petrograd, or January 1918 in Kiev. It did however mark the founding of the legitimacy of the Ukrainian Soviet government, even though this was firmly established only in 1919-20. It was definitely not a revolutionary holiday valorising mass mobilisation but a state holiday promoting 'proletarian statehood' [*proletarskaja gosudarstvennost*].[66] Incidentally, one of the first initiatives of the 1927 commission was to 'address the sister republics, asking them to take part in the jubilee celebration' and to send their own representatives. Telegrams received from institutions all over the USSR were duly kept.[67] Soviet Ukrainian leaders were looking for international recognition, even if this were limited to the boundaries of USSR.

CONCLUSION: IS A TRUE REVOLUTIONARY COMMEMORATION POSSIBLE?

The instrumental character of this new holiday became obvious in 1929 when a new tenth anniversary of Soviet power in Ukraine was defined, corresponding this time to the defeat of Denikin's white troops in Ukraine.[68] Between 1921 and 1927, Ukrainian issues, which had been absent at the beginning, became a concern for Soviet leaders. But this process was a paradoxical one. It meant that commemoration would place great reliance neither on the popular masses nor on a political or cultural background that was purely Ukrainian. On the contrary, it emphasised the bureaucratic aspect of the celebration, praising the essence of power. It meant that leaders considered their legitimacy in an abstract way, the words 'Ukrainian' or 'Proletarian' not requiring any living content. If one can appreciate that 'nationally conscious' Ukrainians utterly disliked the Bolsheviks, what is more astonishing is the lack of concern of the Bolsheviks themselves for feelings among the workers. One could say, as Debord does in *La société du spectacle* (1967), that 'All that once was directly lived has become mere representation'.

COMMEMORATING AN EVENT THAT NEVER OCCURRED

Were other revolutionary commemorations still possible in the early years of the USSR? If so, they took place far from the top party leadership. In Volokhovka, a village fifty kilometres from Kharkov, people gathered in 1929 to celebrate ten years of the commune *Chervona Zorya* (Red Dawn), founded as an attempt to realise communism at the worst point of the civil war.[69] This local proletarian dictatorship in the village endured violence and hunger until 1921. There then began the New Economic Policy, which meant an official lack of interest, if not active disregard, for collectivism. The commune nevertheless survived, and communards were proud to display their achievements over these ten years. Visible on a contemporary newsreel, there were of course official speeches and propaganda,[70] but we can also see youngsters furiously dancing with elders applauding as signs of spontaneous joy and popular participation.

NOTES

1. This research was carried out as a part of the project 'Divided memories, shared memories. Ukraine / Russia / Poland (twentieth-twenty-first centuries): an entangled history', headed by Prof. Korine Amacher (University of Geneva) and supported by the Swiss National Science Foundation (SNSF).
2. 'K pjatiletiju Oktjabr'skoj revoljucii', *Letopis' Revoljucii, Žurnal po izučeniju Istorii Oktjabr'skoj revoljucii I Kommunističeskoj partii Ukrainy,* No. 1, 1922, p5, 'Ot Isparta'.
3. Central State Archive of Public Organisations of Ukraine (CDAGO-U), f. 1, op. 20, d. 748, l. 59 (undated, but probably 16 April 1921). Unless otherwise stated all quoted archival material is from CDAGO-U.
4. See especially f. 1, op. 20, d. 1481 (1922); *Sputnik rabočego na 1925 god* [Almanac], Priboj: Leningrad, 1925, pp9-80.
5. F. 1, op. 20, d. 748, l. 63, 'O prazdonovanii godovščiny sverženija samoderžavija i dnja parižskoj Kommuny' (28 February 1921); f. 1, op. 20, d. 1773, l. 13 (June 1923).
6. F. 1, op. 20, d. 748, l. 151-ob (26 December 1921).

7. *Ibid.*, ll. 31 (c. April 1921), 63.
8. *Ibid.*, ll. 123-6 (28 September 1921).
9. F. 1, op. 20, d. 1451, ll. 1-5 (Agitpropotdel CKRKRP, 'Tezisy dlja agitatorov k pjatoj godovščine Oktjabr'skoj revoljucii', c. September 1922).
10. F. 1, op. 20, d. 748, ll. 13 (15 January 1921), 123 (28 September 1921).
11. F. 1, op. 20, d. 1451, ll. 45-8 (c. summer 1922).
12. About the appeal of the French Revolution in Soviet Russia, see the seminal work of Tamara Kondratieva, *Bolcheviks et Jacobins – Itinéraires des analogies*, Payot: Paris, 1989.
13. Maurice Bernhardt et Henri Cain, *Une nuit de Noël sous la terreur : comédie en 1 acte,* Théâtre Sarah Bernhardt: Paris, 1912; Paul Bourget, *Une nuit de Noël sous la terreur,* H. Daragon: Paris, 1907.
14. F. 1, op. 20, d. 748, ll. 15-16 (c. February 1921).
15. Still in 1933, after years of Ukrainisation and forced rural exodus induced by collectivisation and famine, Ukrainians represented only 48 per cent of the capital's population. See Arakčeev, Magnickij and Bekendorf, 'Xar'kov', *Bol'šaja Sovetskaja Enciklopedija* (1oe izdanie), Vol. 59, 1935.
16. For instance, there were only 10 per cent of locals among the cadres of the Kharkov Party militia (*ChON*) in 1920. See Eric Aunoble, '"Communistes, aux armes !": les unités à destination spéciale (TchON) au sortir de la guerre civile en Ukraine (1920-1924)', *Hispania Nova*, No. 13, 2015, p244.
17. F. 1, op. 20, d. 1451, l. 13 (c. 6-23 September 1922).
18. F. 1, op. 20, d. 1516, l. 153 (c. 12 July 1922).
19. 'Itogi', *Kommunarka Ukrainy*, No. 7-8, July-October 1921, p4.
20. F. 1, op. 20, d. 1449, l. 2 (1 July 1922).
21. F. 1, op. 20, d. 1516, l. 154.
22. F. 1, op. 20, d. 772, l. 19 (6 October 1921).
23. F. 1, op. 20, d. 1489, l. 26 (2 August 1922); f. 1, op. 20, d. 1482, l. 6 (15 August 1922); more generally, on the organisation of such activities, see Alexandre Sumpf, *Bolcheviks en campagne. Paysans et éducation politique dans la Russie des années 1920,* CNRS Éditions: Paris, 2010, pp36-42.
24. For the former, see also Régis Gayraud, 'Les actions de masse des années 1920 en Russie: un nouveau spectacle pour la révolution', *Annales historiques de la Révolution française*, No. 367, janvier-mars 2012, p177.

25. F. 1, op. 20, d. 772, l. 38 (12 October 1921): the Communist Party's Ekaterinoslav city committee asked all district committees to send the list of speakers no later than 18 October.
26. Frederick Corney, *Telling October: Memory and the Making of the Bolshevik Revolution*, Cornell University Press: Ithaca, New York and London, 2004, pp100 sq; Nataliâ Moskovčenko, 'Dvoznačnist' ponjattâ "édynyj deržavnyj arxivnyj fond" (rol' Istpartu v rozvitku arxivnoï spravi Ukraïni)', *Studiï z arxivnoï spravi ta dokumentoznavstva*, Kiev, Vol. 13, 2005, www.archives.gov.ua/Publicat/Studii/Studii_2005.13.01.php, 28 July 2017.
27. F. 1, op. 20, d. 1449, ll. 16-17, 25, 34-5, 39 (March-August 1922); f. 1, op. 20, d. 1773, ll. 6-11 (April 1923).
28. 'K pjatiletiju Oktjabr'skoj revoljucii', *Letopis' Revoljucii, Žurnal po izučeniju Istorii Oktjabr'skoj revoljucii I Kommunističeskoj partii Ukrainy*, No. 1, 1922, p5, 'Ot Isparta'.
29. Mojsej Ravič-Čerkasskij, *Maxno i maxnovščina*, Ekaterinoslav, 1920; *Istorija kommunističeskoj partii (b-ov) Ukrainy*, GIZ: Xar'kov, Ukrainy, 1923.
30. F. 1, op. 20, d. 772, l. 19 (6 October 1921); f. 1, op. 20, d. 2498, ll. 22-26 (25 March 1927); f. 1, op. 20, d. 2919, l. 1 (27 November 1929). As such, he would publicly correct the political 'mistakes' of his colleagues in the early 1930s before being arrested in 1935. But unlike Ravich-Cherkassky who died in custody, Rubach was released and came back to university in 1940 (M. A. Rubač, 'Proty reviziï bil'šovyc'koï sxemy rušijnyx syl ta xarakteru revoljuciï 1917 roku na Ukraïni (Krytyka nacional-demokratyčnoï platformy ta dejakyx uxyliv vid lenins'koï sxemy istoriï proletars'koï revoljuciï)', *Litopys revoljuciï*, No. 5, 1930, pp8-17; O. J. Ščus', 'Rubač Myxajlo Abramovyč', *Encyklopedija istoriï Ukraïny*, Naukova Dumka: Kiev, 2003).
31. F. 1, op. 20, d. 1449, ll. 1 (6 March 1922), 3 (4 September 1922), 54 (27 December 1922).
32. F. 1, op. 20, d. 1773, l. 8 (April 1923); f. 1, op. 20, d. 2022, ll. 1-5 (22 May 1925), 11 (9 June 1925), 12-14, 20-21.
33. F. 1, op. 20, d. 760, l. 99 (19 October 1921).
34. F. 1, op. 20, d. 2498, l. 1 (marked 'Confidential', 9 February 1927); f. 1, op. 20, d. 1857, l. 27 (letter from the GPU plenipotentiary in charge of the movie industry, 6 September 1924).
35. F. 1, op. 20, d. 1449, l. 2 (1 July 1922).

36. F. 1, op. 20, d. 1773, l. 6 (April 1923).
37. F. 1, op. 20, d. 1449, ll. 4 (19 December 1922), 8-16, 28-9 (9 June 1922); f. 1, op. 20, d. 1773, l. 8 ob. (April 23); f. 1, op. 20, d. 1857, l. 20 (2 March 1924).
38. F. 1, op. 20, d. 1451, l. 78 (3 October 1922).
39. Blakytny was a former left-wing Ukrainian socialist-revolutionary and one of the founders of the Ukrainian Communist Party of Borotbysts (*UKP-b*) in 1918, a party which eventually merged with the *KP(b)U* (Communist Party of Ukraine – Bolshevik) in 1920.
40. F. 1, op. 20, d. 1516, ll. 156 sq (c. summer 1923).
41. F. 1, op. 20, d. 760, l. 193 (3 November 1921).
42. F. 1, op. 20, d. 772, l. 48 (20 October 1921); f. 1, op. 20, d. 1451, ll. 24-6 (6 September 1922), 42-3. See also Emilia Koustova, 'Les fêtes révolutionnaires russes entre 1917 et 1920. Des pratiques multiples et une matrice commune', *Cahiers du monde russe*, Vol. 47 No. 4, 2006, pp684-94.
43. *Bjuleten' Istparta* (Russia), No. 1, 1921, p37.
44. F. 1, op. 20, d. 772, l. 48 (20 October 1921); f. 1, op. 20, d. 760, l. 196 (4 November 1921).
45. *Kommunarka Ukrainy*, No. 7-8, 1921, pp5-14.
46. F. 1, op. 20, d. 772, l. 48 (20 October 1921); f. 1, op. 20, d. 1482, l. 119 (c. 1 December 1922).
47. For the solemn session of the Soviet, the intrusion of fake enemies is also planned... F. 1, op. 20, d. 1451, ll. 37-40 (c. September 1922).
48. *Ibid.*, l. 40.
49. Lynn Mally, *Culture of the Future: the Proletkult Movement in Revolutionnary Russia*, University of California Press: Berkeley, 1990, p226; R. Pel'šše, 'Proletkul't', *ŠŠljax do Komunizmu*, Vol. 4 No. 4, 1924, p73.
50. F. 1, op. 20, d. 1451, l. 38.
51. F. 1, op. 20, d. 1482, ll. 114-115.
52. *XV s'ezd Vsesojuznoj Kommunističeskoj partii (b). Dekabr' 1927 goda. Stenografičeskij otčët*, Gosizdat: Moskau-Leningrad, 1928, p1247.
53. N. Semenov, 'Istoryčne značinnja Žovtnevoï revoljuciï', *Ahitacija j propahanda, žurnal ahitpropu CK KP(b)U ta ahitpropu Xarkivs'koho OPK*, Vol. 10 No. 1, 1927, pp9-16; *Kul'trabotnik*, No. 20, 31 October 1927, pp18-23.
54. 'Naučno-političeskaja literatura k 10-letiju Oktjabr'skoj revoljucii', *Kul'trabotnik*, No. 20, 31 October 1927, pp6-9; O. Karpenko,

'Ohljad literatury do Žovtnja na Ukraïni', *Letopis' Revoljucii*, No. 5-6, September-December 1927, pp409-17.
55. F. 1, op. 20, d. 2498, ll. 2-14 (account of the *Istpart*'s activity for 1927).
56. In 1922, the exhibition about the revolution drew a little more than 2000 visitors, and the one that was set up for the party's twenty-fifth anniversary, 8000 visitors (f. 1, op. 20, d. 1773, l. 8 ob. (April 1923); f. 1, op. 20, d. 1857, l. 20 (2 March 1924)).
57. See for instance *Molodyj bil'š'šovyk*, No. 20, October 1927.
58. *Vsesvit*, No. 45, November 1927.
59. *Proletarskaja Pravda* (Kiev), No. 370, 7 November 1922; No. 500, 18 April 1923.
60. For instance, Kievian party historians tried to prove that their city was 'the centre of Ukraine's political life' in 1917 (f. 1, op. 20, d. 2498, l. 19 – c. 27 September 1927).
61. F. 1, op. 20, d. 2492, ll. 68-73 (letters from N.S. Natlax, a veteran who wrote a scenario, 3 May-26 October 1927).
62. *Arsenal*, VUFKU, 1928.
63. F. 1, op. 20, d. 2492, ll. 75-76.
64. V. I. Lenin, 'Manifesto to the Ukrainian People with an Ultimatum to the Ukrainian Rada', *Collected Works*, Progress Publishers: Moscow, Vol. 26, 1972, pp361-3.
65. O. M. Dzûba, V. F. Repryncev & V. F. Verstûk, *Ukraïna vid najdavnišyx časiv do s'ohodennâ – Xronolohičnyj dovidnyk*, Naukova Dumka: Kiev, 1995, p251.
66. F. 1, op. 20, d. 2461, l. 25 (27 December 1927).
67. F. 1, op. 20, d. 2492, ll. 81 (17 December 1927), 83 (19 December 1927); f. 1, op. 20, d. 2461, ll. 15-24.
68. F. 1, op. 20, d. 2919, l. 21 (*Istpart*'s 'Explicative note for the celebration of the 10th anniversary of the defeat of Denikin and the establishment of Soviet power in Ukraine', 1 November 1929).
69. See Éric Aunoble, *'Le Communisme tout de suite!' Le Mouvement des communes en Ukraine soviétique (1919-1920)*, Les Nuits rouges: Paris, 2008.
70. Central State Film, Photo, and Sound Archive of Ukraine (CDKFFA-U), No. 1406 – III (*Kinožurnal*, No. 30/125, 1929).

The Echoes of the Russian October under the State of Siege in Germany, October/November 1918

Ottokar Luban

In late September 1918 the German High Command under the prominent generals Hindenburg and Ludendorff had to concede military defeat to a shocked public,[1] who, due to the nature of official propaganda, were not prepared for such news. This precipitated a fundamental political crisis of confidence in the authorities of the Kaiserreich.[2] It seemed then as if the prophecy made by August Bebel, the most prominent German Social Democrat and a leading figure in the Socialist International, was about to come true: the collapse of capitalism followed by the proletariat and its socialist party seizing power in order to realise a humane, just, and socialist society.[3] But the social-democratic movement in Germany had difficulties exploiting this situation which was favourable to fundamental political and social changes in October and November in 1918. The reason for this was that the party was split.

Before 1914 the Social Democratic Party (*Sozialdemokratische Partei Deutschlands*, SPD) was the largest socialist party in the Socialist International with 982,850 members and 110 deputies in the Reichstag. But since the outbreak of war in August 1914 the parliamentary group (ignoring a resolution of the Socialist International) voted for the war credits; this was true not only in the first chaotic days of the war but in all of the following war years. They also cooperated with the imperial government and the bourgeois parties. Opposition within the party and the parliamentary group to the leadership's stance of loyalty to the government – the so-called 'civil peace' (*Burgfrieden*) – grew from 21 December 1915, when twenty deputies voted against the war credits in the Reichstag. When the opposition held a conference in January 1917 to organise its forces, the party's right wing took the opportunity to expel its rivals. Thus, the opposition was forced to found its own party, the Independent Social Democratic Party (*Unabhängige Sozialdemokratische Partei Deutschlands*, USPD). The largest part of the SPD, under the leadership of Philipp Scheidemann and Friedrich Ebert,[4] kept the majority of the organisation and was, for that reason, known informally as the Majority-SPD (*Mehrheits-SPD*, MSPD) – though officially it retained the name SPD.

The USPD, under the leadership of Hugo Haase[5] – who had been the chairman of the SPD until 1915 – used all available possibilities for anti-war agitation, despite the limits imposed by the state of siege, whether this was in the Reichstag, in the party's newspapers or at party assemblies. Most important of all was the USPD's support for the anti-war mass strikes in April 1917 and January 1918.

From the very beginning of the war, a group of left socialists coalesced around the theorist Rosa Luxemburg and Reichstag deputy and early opponent of the war credits Karl Liebknecht;[6] this radical inner-party circle was known as the Spartacus Group. From the end of 1914, they conducted intensive inner-party agitation against the war credits and, thereafter, they distributed clandestine propaganda calling for revolutionary mass actions. The Spartacus Group joined the USPD at its founding congress in April 1917 as an autonomous faction. It did so as the group's leaders were well aware of their weakness as an organisation. They feared becoming a sect without any influence on the proletarian masses, if they founded another, third, socialist party.[7]

Another grouping on the SPD's pre-war left, which had mainly regional significance, was the Bremen Left Radicals (*Linksradikale*, BLR), which had connections to a further strong group in Hamburg; both were under the influence of Karl Radek and the Bolsheviks,[8] but they also had anarcho-syndicalist tendencies. The Left Radicals called for the foundation of a left-radical party, did not join the USPD, and instead set up their own organisation.[9] Due to the military state of siege, the Spartacus Group and the Bremen and Hamburg Left Radicals suffered under the repression of the imperial authorities, losing several leaders – notably Rosa Luxemburg and Karl Liebknecht – and many supporters who were imprisoned or drafted into the army. These losses were the reason why the radical-left groups, especially the Spartacus Group, remained very weak in the weeks before the outbreak of the German Revolution of 1918. The USPD, too, protested about the regime's repression, such as strict censorship of newspapers, the banning of party meetings, and the political prison sentences, which included imprisoning the party secretary Wilhelm Dittmann for making a speech at a mass-strike rally in February 1918.[10]

All this was in stark contrast to the Majority-SPD and its leaders Ebert and Scheidemann, who had nothing to fear from the imperial authority's repression on account of their loyalty and acceptance of the regime's politics; they were only moderately criticical. Since the middle of 1917, the MSPD entered into cooperation with the parties of the middle classes in an informal committee in the Reichstag. Then, in October 1918, when the first government based on a majority in parliament was formed under the Chancellorship of Prince Max von Baden, the MSPD joined the cabinet dominated by the bourgeois, and used all of its organisational energy to avoid revolution.

THE IMPERIAL AUTHORITIES' LAST ATTEMPTS TO PREVENT REVOLUTION[11]

The Russian embassy in Berlin had already been expelled on 5 November 1918, when the USPD announced five public assemblies for 7 November in the German capital; the events proclaimed 'To the Anniversary of the Russian Revolution'.[12] Several prominent left-wing leaders, like Hugo Haase and Karl Liebknecht, the latter just released from prison on 25 October, hoped to participate. In contrast to the promise of the new liberal government of Chancellor Max von Baden,[13] to relax the state of siege, the military authority banned the USPD meeting. The new Chancellor even went on the evening of 7 November to General von Linsingen,[14] the Commander in Chief for the Berlin military district, to ask him to lift the ban on meetings. But the General refused, referring to the views of the Minister for War, and the Chancellor did not pursue this any further. What this illustrates is that it was not the new parliamentary government but the old military authorities that continued to hold real power in the German capital city.

This was also visible in the streets of Berlin where, until the morning of 9 November, armed soldiers were grouped in fighting positions at crossings, train stations, some factories, and public buildings. The civil telephone and telegram connections between Berlin and the other parts of Germany were interrupted so that newspapers could not get detailed information on the revolutionary development which had broken out in the coastal area of northern Germany. All train connections from Berlin to the north and west of the country were interrupted. Sailors travelling from the harbour cities to the interior of the country, who very often assumed the role of a revolutionary catalyst when they arrived in still quiet cities, could not reach Berlin or, if they did, were arrested at once. By 7 November, the revolutionary wave coming from Kiel and other German coastal cities, including Hamburg and Bremen, has already spread to the western German cities of Cologne, Hannover and Brunswick, and, late on that night, Munich, yet the military authorities and the ruling parties of government, including the MSPD, made every effort to keep revolutionary mass movement away from the capital city of Berlin as the centre and seat of government power.

THE ANTI REVOLUTIONARY AGITATION OF THE MAJORITY-SPD[15]

The MSPD, which had entered the bourgeois coalition government under Chancellor Prince Max von Baden in October, supported the anti-revolutionary goals of these military actions with intensive agitation against revolutionary actions. Already in October, the MSPD executive committee warned the workers not to follow the calls in the radicals' leaflets, which were propaganda for demonstrations and strikes, as this would only disrupt the government's attempts to achieve a quick armistice. The MSPD's central organ, *Vorwärts*, for example, stated on 17 October that its readers should oppose 'actions by irresponsible persons who are confused by Bolshevik revolutionary phrases'.[16]

In the week of 7 November, the MSPD intensified its efforts to prevent revolutionary actions in several appeals carried in its *Vorwärts*. On 6 November, the party's newspaper stated: 'No Russian conditions; forward in unity for the goals of democracy and socialism!'[17]

During those days immediately preceding the revolution, the MSPD leader Friedrich Ebert played the most important anti-revolutionary role. He held daily meetings with MSPD shop stewards in the factories, in which he set out to convince them to resist all revolutionary actions of their radical colleagues in order not to disrupt the party's policy of pursuing further democratic reform, the abdication of the Kaiser, and an immediate armistice. The MSPD and the other parties of government – the Catholic Centre Party, the Progressive People's Party, and the National Liberal Party – tried to keep the revolution from breaking out in the capital city, hoping that the revolutionary movement in northern, western, and southern Germany would expire so that the government of Chancellor Max could continue its work. On 7 November, the day of the first anniversary of the Russian October Revolution, it looked as if the old conservative elites of the German Empire together with their allies in the Reichstag coalition would be able to hold power in the capital city.

THE TACTICS OF THE REVOLUTIONARY LEFT SOCIALISTS

But what did the USPD leaders do after the party assemblies – previously announced for 7 November – were banned? Could they be turned into illegal protest demonstrations, which could then be escalated into revolutionary upheavals? This was the proposal which Karl Liebknecht – after his release from prison on 23 October – made several times at meetings of the revolutionary committee, subsequently known as the 'Revolutionary Shop Stewards'. This committee was an informal grouping, initially comprised only of local officials who were not on the central payroll of the metalworkers' union and who met on an *ad hoc* basis in public houses for discussions after official meetings of the union; they formed a close community and had the solidarity of the workers. Under the leadership of the lathe operator Richard Müller, and in cooperation with the USPD and the Spartacus Group, they were responsible for the strikes in Berlin in June 1916, April 1917, and January 1918.[18]

Since spring 1918, the Revolutionary Shop Stewards, then headed by the plumber Emil Barth,[19] who replaced Richard Müller after he was drafted into the army, felt that they had to prepare not only for another mass strike but for an armed uprising to end the war by any means. But they did not anticipate a revolutionary situation arising in Germany before January 1919. During the summer of 1918, two left-wing members of the USPD executive committee – the Reichstag deputies Ernst Däumig and Georg Ledebour[20] – joined the committee, which from October included additional members of the USPD, as well as Karl Liebknecht, and two additional Spartacists.

The Revolutionary Shop Stewards under Richard Müller and then Emil Barth focused on plans to initiate a well-organised revolutionary mass strike, with armed demonstrations from the plants into the inner city of Berlin, where they would occupy public buildings. Revolutionaries in other cities and regions would then pursue the same tactics on an agreed date. The prerequisite, however, was the workers' readiness for revolutionary mass action. This was recognised at a meeting on the 6 November by the factory delegates to the revolutionary committee, and the date was set for 11 November.[21] This well-planned revolutionary uprising in Berlin was a real proletarian mass movement, which was rooted in the factories and which depended on the voluntary readiness for action of a majority of the workers.

THE GERMAN LEFT AND THE BOLSHEVIKS[22]

In the USPD leadership there were some voices critical of the development of the Russian Revolution; among the most vocal were the long-serving party theorist Karl Kautsky, the Menshevik journalist Alexander Stein, the theorist Rudolf Hilferding, and the former editor-in-chief of *Vorwärts* Heinrich Ströbel.[23] The rank and file, however, was much in favour of the Bolsheviks, as many police reports of party meetings prove.[24] After much debate in party newspapers and at party meetings, there was majority support among party officials at an unofficial conference on 11-12 September 1918 for the Bolshevik policy of realising socialism; the USPD leadership called on all international socialist parties to hinder capitalist governments from disrupting developments in Russia. Although this resolution was relatively moderate, it was banned by the censorship imposed by the military authorities.[25] The secret party conference has remained almost unknown in the historiography, due to the absence of documentation.[26] However, we now have two contemporary Russian sources. Firstly, there is a letter of 16 September 1918 to Lenin by the Bolshevik representative Pjotr Studschka,[27] who was one of the main speakers at the secret USPD conference in Berlin; and secondly, there is a much more detailed report by Studschka in the Bolsheviks' central organ, *Pravda,* on 24 November 1918. Most important was Studschka's presence at the meeting of the Revolutionary Shop Stewards where he felt 'much more at home' than at the USPD conference, as he reported in *Pravda.* Here the Bolsheviks came into contact with Emil Barth, the leader of the Revolutionary Shop Stewards, and were able to arrange financial support through the Soviet ambassador, Adolph Joffe, for the armament of the German Revolutionaries.[28]

The USPD leaders had already publicly declared their readiness to follow the Russian example. In the summer of 1918, the Reichstag deputy Georg Ledebour predicted the revolution would take place in accordance with the Russian model, and party chairman Hugo Haase announced in parliament on 23 October that crowns would fall and be replaced by a republic of the working masses, not of the capitalists – and the masses would stand in solidarity with Soviet Russia.[29]

One observer of these developments in Germany was the Russian ambassador, Adolph Joffe, who came to Berlin at the end of April 1918, after the peace treaty of Brest-Litovsk. In his reports to the Russian Foreign Ministry and especially in personal letters to Lenin, Joffe frequently expressed his disappointment with the USPD – but he had failed to account for the repression of the party's activities by the military and police authorities. Nevertheless Joffe maintained intensive contact with the USPD party leaders and supported its newspaper the *Leipziger Volkszeitung* financially, even penning his own articles for it. But astonishingly, there was no connection with the Revolutionary Shop Stewards before the middle of September 1918.

However, Joffe's contacts with the Berlin-based leaders of the Spartacus Group were much closer, and included the historian Franz Mehring, the former editor of *Vorwärts*, Ernst Meyer, the teachers Käte and Hermann Duncker, and Clara Zetkin, the head of the women's office of the Socialist International and former editor-in-chief of the newspaper *Gleichheit* in Stuttgart.[30] But Joffe was well aware of the weakness of the Spartacists, due to the imprisonment of the group's leaders, Rosa Luxemburg, Karl Liebknecht, and Leo Jogiches,[31] as well as many of their supporters. Joffe not only sponsored the Spartacus Group and its newspapers financially – as he did the Left Radicals in Bremen – he even wrote the resolution of the Spartacus Group conference of 13 October 1918, visible in a letter from Joffe to Lenin, dated 13 October 1918.[32]

THE SPARTACUS LEADERS AND THE BOLSHEVIKS[33]

Joffe very much approved of the journalistic support for the Bolsheviks provided by the Spartacus leaders Franz Mehring and Clara Zetkin. In many Spartacus leaflets, the Russian Revolution was praised and the masses were called on to follow its example. This can be seen, for example, in the pamphlet entitled 'On the anniversary of the socialist revolution in Russia', which intended to support the planned USPD meetings set for 7 November, before they were ultimately banned.[34]

Though there was a general approval of Bolshevik policy among the Spartacus leadership, the majority rejected the 'red terror', as Angelica Balabanova wrote to Lenin on 19 October, after a stay in Berlin.[35] The content of Rosa Luxemburg's later famous critical manuscript on the Russian Revolution, which had been written in September and early October 1918, was unknown for many months even to her closest comrades because, together with her other writings, until the spring of 1919, it had been kept in the hands of a socialist family in Breslau, where Luxemburg had been imprisoned in the fortress. But we also know that Luxemburg was critical of the Bolsheviks from discussion with her Polish comrade Henryk Walecki,[36] during late November and early December 1918, who recorded his discussions with her later on.[37] This shows that even the Spartacus Group, which had the closest connections with the Bolsheviks, held a different position to their Russian comrades, which included support for grassroots democracy whereby revolutionary force should be used only defensively against attacks by the bourgeoisie.[38]

During October, until the expulsion of the Russian embassy on 5 November, the Spartacists had many consultations with Joffe and with Nikolai Bukharin,[39] who was also in Berlin at that time. The Russians encouraged the Spartacists to begin the revolution with street demonstrations instead of concentrating on one big uprising in Berlin as the Revolutionary Shop Stewards had planned. But a Spartacus demonstration near the Reichstag building on 16 October failed miserably: only a few hundred participants took to the streets. The reason for this failure was that the Berlin USPD organisation withdrew its support.

Observing developments in Germany, Joffe was very sceptical about the immediate prospects for revolution. In a letter of 28 October, he speculated that it remained months away.[40] The Spartacist leaders shared his assessment; as late as 5 November, Hermann Duncker commented after receiving the first news from the sailors' mutinies that the situation in Berlin lacked revolutionary promise: 'And what will the Berliners do? Nothing! It's a crying shame'.[41]

THE UNCERTAIN PROSPECTS FOR THE REVOLUTIONARY UPRISING[42]

On 2 November, the majority of the rank and file of the Revolutionary Shop Stewards saw no real readiness for revolutionary mass actions in the Berlin factories and, for this reason, postponed the date for the great uprising in Berlin until 11 November. The messengers who were sent out to provincial towns with information on the date for the uprising also returned to Berlin with the news that most of their left-wing comrades in those cities did not see a favourable situation for revolutionary actions. On the other hand, the encouraging news of the successful, spontaneous revolutionary movement among the sailors reached Berlin. As a consequence of these different sources of information, the situation for the revolutionaries in Berlin on the anniversary of the Russian October Revolution was quite unclear, and it became even more so when, on 8 November, the Berlin police arrested the revolutionary leader Ernst Däumig and confiscated his briefcase with the plans for the 11 November uprising.

The members of the revolutionary committee could then have gone underground and waited until 11 November, or even longer. But although the troops were still on the streets and the revolutionary leaders were scattered into several groups in different locations in the city, all continuing to fear arrests, militants spontaneously decided to call the uprising for the next day, 9 November. To this end, they published and distributed two leaflets. Emil Barth even succeeded in organising a meeting of the rank and file, at which he gave orders for the armed mass demonstrations from the factories to the inner city.

On the morning of 9 November, the revolutionary leaders on the one side and the governing powers of the old order, including the MSPD, on the other, were uncertain as to whether the workers would follow the call for revolutionary mass demonstrations. In the event, they did, and this was aided by the detailed preparations made by the Revolutionary Shop Stewards and their intensive agitation which encouraged the masses to leave the factories and form armed demonstrations moving towards the inner city; en route, they convinced soldiers in their barracks to join them and to occupy public buildings. At noon on 9 November, it was clear that the revolutionary workers had seized power in Berlin. The main task of the German revolution had been achieved. In her standard work on German Social Democracy, the historian Susanne Miller emphasised the crucial importance of the revolutionary events in the capital city, which were 'decisive for the destiny of the revolution'.[43]

THE SO-CALLED 'BOLSHEVIK DANGER'

West German historiography in the 1950s was dominated by the opinion that the main task for the MSPD and the bourgeois parties during the November Revolution was to hold back the Bolshevik danger associated with fear of chaos, civil war, and dictatorship. This argument was used by historians to justify MSPD cooperation with the old imperial authorities and to explain the party's neglect of more vigorous democratic reforms of the old state institutions. Even the MSPD's alliance with the military and the reactionary *Freikorps* in order to suppress left socialists in 1919, which brought many victims among workers, was defended with reference to this argument. Then, at the 1964 'Congress of the Historians of the Federal Republic' the defence-against-Bolshevism argument was superseded in the light of new archival-based research; now, West German historians argued that the radicals had been too weak to seize power and build a socialist society. At the same time, the majority of West German historians also identified that there had been the possibility of introducing more crucial democratic and social reforms at the beginning of the Weimar Republic, a 'third way' between capitalism and socialism.[44] Since the end of the 1960s, most historians have subscribed to another view: that the MSPD together with the USPD could have realised at least some deeper democratic and social reform if they had put more energy into these issues.[45]

In the debate on the 'Bolshevik danger' – despite its obvious relevance – it is rarely mentioned that all of the German socialist groups, even those on the far-left fringe of the Bremen Left Radicals, and prominent figures like Rosa Luxemburg, subscribed to highly autonomous political views, even although they supported Bolshevik policy in general. The Bremen Radicals – including the Hamburg Group, who showed greatest support for Bolsheviks – did not support Lenin on organisational issues: the groups' leadership propagated a united organisation of socialist party and union, the so-called 'Unity Organisation' (*Einheitsorganisation*).[46] Rosa Luxemburg and the Spartacus Group rejected any kind of minority socialist government and the practice of political repression and terror. Proletarian terror was held to be permissible only as a defence against counter-revolutionary attack. Instead, socialist society was thought to be realisable only in the context of political freedom with the broad, active participation of the proletarian masses.[47] Thus the 'Bolshevik danger' was in all reality a spectre, which had already been used by the MSPD in the November Revolution 1918 and thereafter, to justify their suppression of the left socialists' pursuit of more ambitious democratic and social goals.[48]

THE INFLUENCE OF THE BOLSHEVIK REVOLUTION

Were these revolutionary events in Germany an echo of the October Revolution of 1917 in Russia? Of course we cannot tell the extent to which the Russian example contributed to revolutionary developments in Germany. Certainly, the immense number of victims during the long war, and starvation which at times approached the proportions of famine, contributed most to the growing general dissatisfaction. This peaked when, in the first October days of 1918, the German military leaders had to admit military defeat. For the German population, which until September 1918 had been subjected to government propaganda that victory was assured, impending defeat came as a shock, and it undermined confidence in the imperial authorities.

What the Russian example did do was offer hope and encouragement that Germany could achieve peace without and against the imperial generals and the monarchical order of the Kaiserreich. With the sudden emergence of the 'Workers' and Soldiers' Councils' the German masses did follow the Russian role model and this happened despite the lack of media attention to it: the MSPD scarcely mentioned the Councils in their newspapers. When they did, it was hostile. A very short time before the November Revolution, in a statement of 21 October, the MSPD even accused the Councils of being part of the dictatorship in Soviet Russia.[49] Yet, despite this type of condemnation, the MSPD's members and supporters throughout Germany participated in the Soldiers' and Workers' Councils, including acting to set up Councils themselves.[50] For the German workers, the Russian model of Workers' and Soldiers' Councils had become a symbol of a future peace and social change. The institution of the Councils also had a great significance for the relative – if temporary – stabilisation of revolutionary power. Without the Councils, the restoration of the old power structures – as is often lamented in the historiography – would have come sooner and been more completely.

The central commemoration of the Russian October Revolution, with the planned seven USPD rallies in Berlin on 7

November 1918, could still be banned by the old authorities. But the revolutionary wave had already reached the harbour cities of the Baltic coast and the North Sea and, beyond them, Cologne, Hannover, Brunswick, and even Munich – owing to the initiatives of the USPD leader Kurt Eisner – and it spread over the coming days to Düsseldorf, Frankfurt-am-Main, Magdeburg, Leipzig, Dresden, Breslau, and beyond.[51] Despite the MSPD's intensive anti-revolutionary agitation and its attempts at intimidation with the military presence on Berlin's streets, aiming to hold back the revolution from the capital city, the revolution nevertheless arrived. The left socialist leaders and the proletarian masses had kept their revolutionary powder dry for the planned armed uprising on the 11 November.

When it looked as if the old authorities would begin measures to suppress Berlin's revolutionary leaders by arresting Ernst Däumig on 8 November, the insurgents acted to begin the upheaval in the capital on the morning of the 9 November, which led to the final successful seizure of power by the proletarian masses. The MSPD in Berlin formed a revolutionary government with the USPD on 10 November, with the promise of changing the situation of their proletarian supporters with this newly won power.

Looking at all organisational levels of the left-socialist movement – its leaders, officials and the rank and file – we can recognise that, in general terms, the October Revolution in Russia was an encouraging example for the German revolutionaries. They achieved an armistice on 11 November and fighting ended, the Kaiser abdicated and the Princely Houses fell in the states of the German Empire, and Workers' and Soldiers' Councils were spontaneously formed. Yet, this new governmental system lasted only a little more than two months – until the election of the National Assembly on 19 January 1919.

In place of the Kaiserreich and a parliamentary system subordinate to the monarch, Germany now had a democracy – but, due to the strong anti-revolutionary efforts of the MSPD, not as a basic democratic council system, but as a bourgeois parliamentary democracy without any real fundamental social and economic change.

NOTES

1. Paul von Hindenburg (1847-1934): field marshal and head of the High Command between 1916-1918. Erich Ludendorff (1865-1937): a general and Hindenburg's deputy between 1916-1918. Under the state of siege, they held both military and governmental power in Germany during the last two war years.
2. Volker Ullrich, *Die nervöse Großmacht. Aufstieg und Untergang des deutschen Kaiserreichs 1871-1918*, Fischer Verlag: Frankfurt am Main, 2010, pp557-567.
3. August Bebel (1840-1913): chairman of the SPD between 1892-1913. Anneliese Beske und Eckhard Müller (eds), *August Bebel – Ausgewählte Reden und Schriften*, Band 7/1: Reden und Schriften 1899 bis 1905, de Gruyter Verlag: München, 1997, p296; Anneliese Beske und Eckhard Müller (eds), *August Bebel – Ausgewählte Reden und Schriften*, Band 8/2: Reden und Schriften 1906 bis 1913, de Gruyter Verlag: München, 1997, p576.
4. Philipp Scheidemann (1865-1939): chairman of the SPD between 1911-1918 and chairman of the party's parliamentary faction. Friedrich Ebert (1871-1925): chairman of the SPD between 1913-1918, and of the SPD's parliamentary faction between 1916-1918.
5. Hugo Haase (1863-1919): SPD chairman between 1911-1916, also of the SPD parliamentary group until December 1915, chairman of the USPD from 1917 to March 1919, also of its parliamentary faction.
6. Rosa Luxemburg (1871-1919): leading socialist theorist before 1914, head of the Spartacus Group, imprisonment from February 1915 to February 1916, and from July 1916 to 8 November 1918. Karl Liebknecht (1871-1919): Reichstag deputy, head of the Spartacus Group, imprisonment from May 1916 to 23 October 1918. Both were murdered by the Freikorps on 15 January 1919.
7. David W. Morgan, *The Socialist Left and the German Revolution. A History of the German Independent Social Democratic Party, 1917-1922*, Cornell University Press: Ithaca, New York, 1975, pp31 ff;

Pierre Broué, *The German Revolution 1917-23*, Haymarket Books: Chicago, 2006, pp43 ff; Susanne Miller, *Die Bürde der Macht. Die deutsche Sozialdemokratie 1918-1920*, Verlag Droste: Düsseldorf, 1978, pp51 ff.

8. Karl Radek (1885-1939): Polish journalist and left-wing politician, who was active in Germany, Switzerland, and later in the Soviet Union. During the war he supported Lenin and became a key Bolshevik leader in running policy in Germany.
9. For Bremen, see Gerhard Engel, *Johann Knief – ein unvollendetes Leben*, Karl Dietz Verlag: Berlin, 2011, especially p319; for both groups, see Paul Frölich, *Im radikalen Lager. Politische Autobiographie 1890-1921*, Basis Druck: Berlin, 2013, especially pp125 ff, pp141 ff.
10. Wilhelm Dittmann (1874-1954): SPD Reichstag deputy between 1917-1922 and secretary of the USPD central committee, imprisonment from February to October 1918.
11. For the following, see my detailed study: Ottokar Luban, 'Die Novemberrevolution 1918 in Berlin. Eine notwendige Revision des bisherigen Geschichtsbildes', *JahrBuch für Forschungen zur Geschichte der Arbeiterbewegung*, No. 1, 2009, pp54-78.
12. See the leaflet with the announcement in Ingo Materna and Hans-Joachim Schreckenbach (eds), *Dokumente aus geheimen Archiven. Berichte des Berliner Polizeipräsidenten zur Stimmung und Lage der Bevölkerung in Berlin, 1914-1918*, Band 4, Hermann Böhlaus Nachf.: Weimar, 1987, Dokument 15.
13. Max von Baden (1867-1929): chancellor of the first parliamentary government of the Kaiserreich from 4 October to 9 November 1918, who gave the chancellorship to the SPD chairman Friedrich Ebert on 9 November 1918.
14. Alexander Adolf August Karl von Linsingen (1850-1935): lieutenant general, commander-in-chief and governor of the Berlin region with absolute governmental power from June 1918 to 9 November 1918.
15. For the following see Luban, *op. cit.*, pp55-78 (especially pp55-58).
16. *Vorwärts*, 18 October 1918.
17. *Vorwärts*, 6 November 1918.
18. Richard Müller (1880-1943): see Ralf Hoffrogge, *Working Class Politics in the German Revolution. Richard Müller, the Revolutionary Shop Stewards and the Origins of the Council Movement*, Brill: Chicago, 2015, especially pp27-60.
19. Emil Barth (1879-1941).

20. Ernst Däumig (1866-1922); Georg Ledebour (1850-1947).
21. Luban, *op. cit.*, pp62-67; Morgan, *op. cit.*, pp107-112; Hoffrogge, *op. cit.*, pp27-60.
22. Morgan, *op. cit.*, pp98-103; Ottokar Luban, 'Russische Bolschewiki und deutsche Linkssozialisten am Vorabend der deutschen Novemberrevolution. Beziehungen und Einflussnahme', *Jahrbuch für Historische Kommunismusforschung*, 2009, pp283-298.
23. Karl Kautsky (1854-1938); Alexander Stein (1881-1948); Rudolf Hilferding (1877-1941); Heinrich Ströbel (1869-1944).
24. Landesarchiv Berlin, A Pr. Br. Rep. 030, Nr. 15822, folder 230, 230 back; Nr. 16005, folder 301f [concerning Berlin]; Niedersächsisches Staatsarchiv Wolfenbüttel, 133, Neu 1793, no folder number (der Kriminal-Inspektor, Cöln, 4 November 1918); *ibid.*, no folder number (Abschrift, Politische Abteilung, Düsseldorf, 4 November 1918); *ibid.*, 12 A neu, Fb. 5, Nr. 6234, folder 150f [Brunswick].
25. Leo Stern (ed.), *Die Auswirkungen der großen sozialistischen Oktoberrevolution auf Deutschland*, Rütten & Loening: Berlin [Ost], 1959, pp1563-64.
26. Robert F. Wheeler, *USPD und Internationale. Sozialistischer Internationalismus in der Zeit der Revolution*, Ullstein Verlag: Frankfurt, 1975, p41, p301 note 145; Morgan, *op. cit.*, p102 note 86.
27. Pjotr Studschka (1865 -1932): member of the Soviet government, representative of the Bolsheviks.
28. 'The German "Independent Revolutionaries"', *Pravda*, No. 255, 24 November 1918. Further on Studschka's letter to Lenin, 16 September 1918, with less information, in Hermann Weber, Jakov Drabkin and Bernhard H. Bayerlein (eds), *Deutschland, Russland, Komintern. II. Dokumente (1918-1943)*, Teilband 1 [1918-1933], de Gruyter Verlag: Berlin, 2015, pp47-50, www.degruyter.com/view/product/212875, 28 July 2017. On the financing of armaments, see Luban, 'Die Novemberrevolution', pp67-70.
29. Miller, *op. cit.*, p61.
30. Franz Mehring (1846-1919). Ernst Meyer (1887-1930); due to lung disease he could not be drafted to the army, but was jailed several times for his political activities. Käte Duncker (1871-1953), speaker for the Spartacus Group at the SPD central conference (*Reichskonferenz*) in September 1916, head of the group in cooperation with Jogiches in summer 1916, connections for the Spartacus Group with the Socialist Youth movement. Hermann Duncker (1874-1960): Spartacus Group

leading member from May to October 1918. Clara Zetkin (1857-1933).
31. Leo Jogiches (1867-1919): main leader of the Spartacus Group, summer 1916 to March 1918.
32. German translation in Weber et al. (eds), *op. cit.*, pp47-50.
33. For the following, see Luban, 'Russische Bolschewiki', pp289-297; see also Ottokar Luban, 'Rosa Luxemburg's Critique of Lenin's Ultra Centralistic Party Concept and of the Bolshevik Revolution', *Critique*, Vol. 40 No. 3, 2012, pp357-366.
34. Institut für Marxismus-Leninismus beim ZK der SED (ed.), *Dokumente und Materialien zur Geschichte der deutschen Arbeiterbewegung*, Series II 1914-1948, Band 2, November 1917-December 1918, Dietz: Berlin [Ost] 1957, pp307–315.
35. Russian State Archives for Social and Political History (RGASPI), f. 5, op. 3, d. 80, folder 2 back.
36. Henryk Walecki (1877-1938): Polish left socialist, founding member of the Polish Communist Party.
37. RGASPI, f. 495, op. 124, d. 539, folder 42 back (handwritten report by Henryk Walecki in German).
38. Luban, 'Rosa Luxemburg's Critique', pp357-365; Sobhanlal Datta Gupta, *The Socialist Vision and the Silenced Voices of Democracy: New Perspectives*, Part I, Rosa Luxemburg, Seribaan: Bakhrahat, 2015, pp25-33.
39. Nikolai Bukharin (1888-1938): leading economic theorist of the Bolsheviks.
40. Archive for the Foreign Policy of the Russian Federation, f. 4, m. 70, d. 990, folder 94 f.
41. Heinz Deutschland (ed.), *Käte und Hermann Duncker. Ein Tagebuch in Briefen (1894-1953)*, Dietz Verlag: Berlin, 2016, letter to his daughter Hedwig, 5 November 1918.
42. For the following, see Luban, 'Novemberrevolution', pp62-67, pp70-74.
43. Miller, *op. cit.*, p79.
44. Wolfgang Niess, *Die Revolution von 1918/19 in der deutschen Geschichtsschreibung. Deutungen von der Weimarer Republik bis ins 21. Jahrhundert*, de Gruyter Verlag: Berlin, 2013, pp164-201, pp207-214.
45. *Ibid.*, pp231-416.
46. Engel, *op. cit.*, pp304-306.
47. Luban, 'Rosa Luxemburg's Critique', pp357-366.
48. Niess, *op. cit.*, pp82-90.

49. 'The Russian revolution swept away democracy and replaced it with the dictatorship of the Workers' and Soldiers' Councils. The Social Democratic Party unequivocally rejects Bolshevik theory and methods for Germany and declares its commitment to democracy', *Vorwärts*, 21 October 1918, quoted in Broué, *op. cit.*, p130; Eberhard Kolb, *Die Arbeiterräte in der deutschen Innenpolitik 1918-1919*, Ullstein Verlag: Frankfurt am Main, 1978, pp29-30.
50. *Ibid.*, pp81-82, pp86-87.
51. *Ibid.*, pp83-97.

Celebrating October: The Transnational Commemorations of the Tenth Anniversary of the Soviet Union in Weimar Germany

Kasper Braskén

> Hundreds of people have come here as delegates to the Tenth Anniversary of October. These people who have been sent from various parts of the world belong to different social strata, to different political orientations (only 15 per cent of them are Communists). Almost all of them represent organisations, groups, movements, and bodies of people. Their object is to see for themselves the positive results of the Russian Revolution.[1]

These were the opening words of the French author, communist, anti-fascist, and Soviet sympathiser Henri Barbusse at 'the congress of witnesses' in Moscow on 10 November 1927. The event was perceived as a 'Congress of Friends' that would result in the establishment of a worldwide network of Friends of the Soviet Union organisations. According to Barbusse's report, all international delegates attending the congress had had 'full freedom' to study and inspect the results of the revolution. Consequently, what they had witnessed should have opened their eyes and made them realise how badly informed the public in Europe and the world were when it came to understanding and appreciating the 'material and ideological consequences' of October. Barbusse could not have expressed more clearly his belief in the meaning of the October Revolution. At last, a 'sixth part of the globe has been totally reorganised by and for the exploited, by and for the proletarians of town and countryside, by and for the oppressed populations and races'.[2]

This Congress of Friends was the highpoint of a long effort by the Communist International (Comintern), the International Workers' Relief (*Internationale Arbeiterhilfe*, IAH), and the All-Union Society for Cultural Ties Abroad (VOKS) to stage a spectacular international ten-year jubilee celebration of October. While the activities of VOKS have been discussed in the works of Michael David-Fox and Jean-François Fayet, the aim here is to analyse the commemorations organised by the German communist Willi Münzenberg, the International Workers' Relief, and the Comintern.[3] VOKS was a Soviet governmental institution based in Moscow that was mainly concerned with inviting prominent foreigners to the Soviet Union and forming cultural ties with the wider world. The IAH, on the other hand, was based in Berlin and belonged to the transnational world of the Comintern with the mission of organising broad international solidarity campaigns for the workers and the oppressed around the world. Unlike VOKS, the IAH organised a wide range of solidarity campaigns that were not directed toward the Soviet Union. These included food relief for workers during major strikes and lockouts, aid campaigns to working-class victims following natural calamities, organising children's homes for poor working-class families, and the creation of major solidarity festivals and cultural events. The above mentioned Friends of the Soviet Union organisation was a direct result of Münzenberg's efforts to mobilise sympathy for the Soviet Union in the western countries during the October celebrations of 1927. Likewise, it was a way to channel new and existing supporters and sympathisers, who were not members of communist parties, into an organised form. Münzenberg played a key role in the planning and framing of the celebrations, which included the sending of 1000 delegates to Moscow, and the showcasing of Soviet cultural, social, and political achievements to a broad public in Germany. The celebrations were framed within a larger context of working-class internationalism and strove in the process to sell the idea of the Soviet Union as the 'fatherland' of all the workers of the world.

Under Münzenberg's leadership, since 1921, the IAH had organised major international solidarity campaigns in the western world, and especially in Germany. The organisation consisted of a mixture of communist, socialist, and 'politically unorganised' workers and intellectual supporters.[4] Through its activities, the IAH was shaping a transnational community of workers, intellectuals, and artists in the west who shared a positive and sympathetic image of the Soviet Union.[5] The aim of the celebrations launched by the IAH was not to make it into a communist affair, but to make the commemorations a broad cultural and political spectacle that would capture the interest of a wider public. The central question considered here is therefore: how was the USSR made into a cause worth celebrating beyond limited circles of communist party members?

It is argued here that the celebrations enabled the creation and strengthening of civil society-based transnational networks, especially between Germany and the Soviet Union, as German workers travelled to Moscow in workers' delegations to participate in the 'showcasing of the Great October Revolution'. Simultaneously, as part of the campaign, Soviet cultural accomplishments were transferred to Germany, as, for example, when the Soviet agitprop troupe 'Blaue Blusen' (the Blue Shirts) toured Germany for several months. The IAH's many illustrated publications such as the *AIZ (Arbeiter Illustrierte Zeitung)*, *Mahnruf* and its proletarian film companies Mezhrabpom and Prometheus

Film also make this a significant case for the history of the echoes of the commemorations. It can provide an answer to how and why the celebration of the Soviet Union could be developed into a broader movement, and into a moment of transnational interconnectedness and shared identity, which was centred on concepts of revolution, social change, and an internationalism of the exploited and oppressed.

MÜNZENBERG AND THE STAGING OF THE TEN-YEAR ANNIVERSARY

Before analysing the commemorations in Moscow and Germany in 1927, we need to take a step back to 1926, when the first ideas for the ten-year commemorations were discussed within the international communist movement. The section that follows will reveal some of the dynamics of the international preparations that caused a heated conflict between the IAH and VOKS. It further demonstrates, through new archival findings, the central role played by Münzenberg, who from the campaign's very beginning, led and shaped the preparations of the international celebrations. In the autumn of 1926, Münzenberg explained to the high-ranking Comintern official Otto Wille Kuusinen that he thought it one of his life missions [*Lebensaufgabe*] to organise a great campaign for Russia in 1927. Münzenberg subsequently wrote a first draft campaign plan for the celebrations and commemorations in November 1926, which was discussed with the highest officials within the Comintern including Kuusinen, Bukharin, the delegation of the German Communist Party (KPD), and lastly even with Soviet party leader Viacheslav Molotov in Moscow.[6]

A campaign plan was finalised but, typically for the Comintern, official approval for the plan was delayed. On 9 January 1927, Münzenberg complained to the Comintern that they were already running very late with the campaign's launch.

The ten-year celebrations were not planned only for October-November but for the entire year. What Münzenberg envisaged was that they should first roll out articles on the January revolution of 1905 that could be published in the left socialist and sympathising press. The second step was to report on the events in Russia in February 1917 and the meaning of the Kerensky period for Russia and the proletariat. In Münzenberg's vision of the campaign, the articles were to be published with hitherto unseen pictures from these revolutionary moments.[7] However, things were moving slowly on the Russian side and, as late as 25 January 1927, he was notified that pictures on the February revolution of 1917 could be obtained from the 'Museum of the Revolution' in Moscow if they could pay for the copies.[8]

One might have assumed that the anniversary campaign would be directly accepted by all communist parties. However, many were not happy that the Comintern was rolling out international campaigns through Münzenberg's International Workers' Relief organisation. This is also an important issue when dealing with the transnational organisation of the tenth anniversary; for example, Münzenberg presented the plan at a meeting of the Central Committee (CC) of the KPD in Berlin on 24 January 1927. Münzenberg described the idea to use the jubilee to win over broad groups in the west who were not party members, but who potentially had a great sympathy for the Soviet Union. The plan was to involve them in the support of the Soviet Union through the establishment of so called Soviet Friendship Clubs (*Klubs der Freunde Sowjetrusslands*).[9] However, when Münzenberg presented the campaign plan to the KPD, his ideas were met with a sceptical response. The KPD leadership had openly questioned if this was really in accordance with the decisions of the Comintern, or whether the Comintern even welcomed any such campaign. All the members of the KPD's CC declared that they knew nothing of such a plan. Münzenberg, in his own words, stood there alone as the others believed that he was pushing his own schemes rather than the Comintern's. The KPD leadership insisted that the matter be put on ice until confirmation came from Moscow. Accordingly, Münzenberg urgently requested the Comintern to confirm that he was following their line and had a mandate to lead the campaign for the tenth anniversary. Most importantly, he had been given a mandate to form friendship clubs in Germany, the USA, Britain, and Czechoslovakia that, according to his own estimate, could potentially attract hundreds of thousands of members.[10]

One of Münzenberg's fiercest critics within the German communist movement was Eduard Fuchs, at that time a leading character behind the *Gesellschaft der Freunde des neuen Russland* (The Association of the Friends of the New Russia) that published the journal *Das neue Rußland* (*The New Russia*). Paradoxically when the association was founded in the summer of 1923, Münzenberg had been integrally connected to its establishment and saw it as a way of linking the movement to bourgeois intellectuals, authors, artists, and scientists.[11] In 1927, it was Fuchs who was Münzenberg's main critic at the KPD's CC meeting on 24 January. In letters to Clara Zetkin and Olga Kameneva of VOKS, Fuchs expressed his fury at Münzenberg's way of introducing the idea of the Soviet Friendship Clubs and related publications into Germany. These were seen as direct attacks against the older organisation and its journal, and Fuchs believed it impossible to have two identical publications and seemingly identical friendship organisations in Germany.

What seems to have irritated several leading communists was that, by the time the KPD's CC and Fuchs were informed of Münzenberg's plans, everything had already been set in motion. Three public meetings in Germany had been officially announced by Münzenberg for the beginning of February, to mobilise support for the defence of the Soviet Union and against the increasing war danger. These meetings were intended to conclude with the establishment of the first Soviet Friendship Clubs. Typically for Münzenberg, he had finalised these plans with the leaders of the Comintern while keeping the KPD's CC out of the loop until it was time to implement them. According to Fuchs, he was expecting to report on speedy results, impressive mass meetings, and large print runs of his new journal. However, Fuchs continued, this would only impress 'the stupid and unsuspecting', and there was no possibility of winning over the German petty bourgeoisie or intellectuals for an active fight for the Soviet Union. Those in the know would notice that the people supporting the new Friendship Clubs were the same as were involved in other 'Münzenberg organisations' such as the League against Imperialism and the IAH. Moreover, the working-class supporters of the new organisation would be recruited from the ranks of the KPD and the communist combat league *Rote Frontkämpferbund* (Red Front Fighters' League). As Fuchs saw it, all of Münzenberg's 'successes' were nothing but Potemkin villages, and as soon as the new clubs met, everyone would know that they were nothing but the progeny of the communist party. Fuchs claimed here that his own friendship society had in reality penetrated the ranks of the bourgeoisie and was making a real impact. Though Münzenberg could as usual produce a long list of familiar names, Fuchs maintained that he would be unable to find a single reliable and prominent bourgeois supporter.[12]

Following this heavy criticism, Münzenberg wrote in disbelief to Moscow asking rhetorically if the Comintern was really willing to abstain from organising 100,000 workers in the new Soviet Friendship Clubs due to the complaints of a dozen intellectuals such as Fuchs. If this was the case, he retorted that he would of course fall in line.[13] Nevertheless, Münzenberg in his disbelief pressed the Comintern to quickly inform the communist parties that his actions had Comintern approval, and even wrote to Bukharin to remind him of how, in conversations in Moscow, he had given the campaign his full blessing. According to Münzenberg, Bukharin had asked him what kind of assistance he required, and Münzenberg had allegedly responded: 'simply that you do not interfere'.[14]

Although space does not allow a detailed discussion of the deliberations in Moscow, the main emerging problem was caused by a conflict between VOKS and Münzenberg's IAH. As leader of VOKS, Kameneva shared Fuchs' great irritation at Münzenberg's plans for Soviet Friendship Clubs. Parallel to Münzenberg, VOKS had prepared a competing plan for the jubilee celebrations that Manuilsky presented to the Comintern's political secretariat on 4 February 1927, arguing that this moment was the greatest opportunity to use the anniversary to form a worldwide united-front movement.[15] The political secretariat was suddenly confronted with two separate plans for the celebrations. On the one hand, there was Münzenberg's, already approved in principle by the Comintern's enlarged executive, which centred on inviting international delegations of 'sympathisers' (including both workers and intellectuals) to Moscow for a world Congress of Friends. On the other hand, there was now a second plan, presented by Manuilsky, that wished to invite mainly workers to a congress in Moscow. The problem with this, according to the discussions in Moscow, was regarding which organisations should be invited from Germany, and how these were to guarantee that they would not send workers hostile to the Soviet Union. This would need some sort of clause preventing them from sending agents of the bourgeoisie disguised as 'sympathising' workers.[16] This shows how seriously the upcoming celebrations were taken in the Comintern and how important it seemed that the celebrations should not be abused or distorted by critics of the Soviet Union.

Another matter was the organisation of international witnesses to the celebrations in the form of delegations. Was it more important to have witnesses at the celebrations in Moscow on 7 November, or that the delegation visit the USSR beforehand, so that they could tell of the USSR's achievements in their respective home countries during anniversary celebrations? Alfred Kurella of the Comintern's agitprop department argued that it would be useful to invite a part of the delegations for the summer of 1927, so that they would have time to return to their native countries and participate in the international celebrations of October there.

A decisive moment in the discussions occurred when Bukharin turned against Manuilsky's plan and argued that it needed to be realised much more broadly than simply for workers and should extend to a broad range of sympathisers. Echoing Münzenberg's views, Bukharin insisted that it would be a significant mistake if the celebration appeared as something planned and organised from Moscow rather than as a spontaneous movement spreading around the world. For this purpose they needed organisations such as the IAH, and thus Münzenberg's plan of forming a loosely organised network of Friendship Clubs seemed to Bukharin the most favourable way to proceed if they wanted to include intellectuals and social democrats, who would never join purely communist organisations. Communists were not supposed to take a centre-stage in these clubs and committees for the Soviet Union, but to remain secluded in the background. Though their first target was, of course, workers, they also needed the support of intellectuals and other groups, who, according to Bukharin, could have a destabilising effect on imperialism even though they were by no means revolutionaries.[17]

Eventually, on 4 February, the Comintern confirmed to Münzenberg that he was indeed to have charge of the Friendship Clubs and the sending of a so-called intellectual delegation to the Soviet Union.[18] After months of waiting, Münzenberg's plans for the commemoration of the tenth anniversary were thus finally discussed by the political secretariat at the beginning of February

1927. Significantly, the Comintern decided, in accordance with Münzenberg's original plan, that a set of delegations from various proletarian organisations were to be invited to Moscow to participate in an international congress there. Münzenberg's idea of forming Friendship Clubs was also supported and communist parties were to be instructed to support the initiative in every way possible. To avoid further delays, on 9 February, the Comintern authorised Münzenberg to begin implementing the plan with all the forces at his disposal.[19] To an extent this was then done, though other campaigns and initiatives stood in the way, notably the Brussels congress of 10-15 February 1927 at which the League against Imperialism and for National Independence (LAI) was formed under Münzenberg's leadership.[20]

On 19 March, the Comintern noted to Münzenberg that it had dispatched instructions to all communist parties regarding the celebrations of 1927.[21] In his first thorough report on the campaign on 26 March, Münzenberg confirmed that it had been severely hampered by the lack of instructions from Moscow to the communist parties, who had consequently falsely believed that it was a campaign planned and initiated by the IAH. In most countries, the communist parties had done little in the matter, in some countries nothing, and in others the IAH's initiative had even been rejected.[22] Somewhat paradoxically, it seems that as the IAH was pushing forward with an independent and much broader campaign plan to celebrate October, the communist parties were unenthusiastic to get involved. These arrangements were a great victory for Münzenberg and the IAH, and a confirmation of his key role within the Comintern hierarchy. This empowered him with vast new resources that were now channelled to the IAH instead of to the communist parties.

Despite Münzenberg's broader approach, it was not self-evident to the campaign's target group why the ten-year anniversary was worth celebrating. Active propaganda was therefore needed that explicitly elaborated on the *meaning* and *relevance* of October, not only from a communist perspective, but from the international Left more broadly. Münzenberg wrote to the Comintern that the anniversary campaign would only appeal to the broad masses if it was connected to current issues like the national liberation struggle in China or the impending imperialist war. This was also the reason why he had launched the campaign in Germany with the slogan 'Against a new war, for China and for Soviet Russia'. In the IAH press, the campaign took the form of positive articles on the USSR, and in the *AIZ*, two pages of every issue were dedicated to the campaign.[23]

When planning the commemoration, Münzenberg was convinced that two seemingly separate campaigns had to be merged: 'Ten years of Soviet Russia' and 'Against the rising war danger'.[24] To Münzenberg it was clear that the main ingredient in the effort to win over supporters was the rising war danger.[25] By late January, he was calling it the campaign for 'Ten years of Soviet Russia and for peace'.[26] By the beginning of February, it was 'Ten years of Soviet Russia and against new wars against Soviet Russia'. As a first effort to form a new international solidarity movement with the Soviet Union, Münzenberg reported that the IAH had started collecting names of intellectuals who were prepared to demonstrate public solidarity with the USSR, and who at the same time were taking a stand against British warmongering.[27] The Comintern similarly noted to the KPD in April 1927 that it was important to remember that the idea went far beyond the obvious necessity to celebrate the anniversary, and had to be integrally connected to the ongoing political situation in Germany. Although the German bourgeoisie had made a complete turn to the west, there were, as well as the workers, the petty bourgeoisie and a part of the intelligentsia who were critical of these developments. It was believed within the Comintern that these elements could be influenced to sympathise with the

Soviet Union and perhaps help steer German politics away from an anti-Soviet alliance with France and Britain.[28] In this way the transnational movement had clear political objectives concerning inter-state relations in Europe.

The campaign in Germany took two different directions. On the one hand, there were the emerging Soviet Friendship Clubs, while on the other hand the KPD was heavily involved between May and November 1927. The political direction of the KPD's campaign in Germany was handled by a special commission comprising seven leading communists including Ernst Thälmann, Walter Ulbricht, Franz Dahlem, and Münzenberg. Its objectives were spelled out in three interlinked points. First, it had to be realised that the Soviet Union was the first proletarian state and the centre of the international revolution. The defence of the Soviet Union against world imperialism was consequently the duty of all class conscious workers, all working peasants, and all those who wished to secure peace and the progress of humanity. Secondly, and somewhat more controversially, it was demanded that all workers realise the importance of Leninism for the defeat of imperialism and for the victory of the proletariat. Lastly, all had to realise that the liberation struggle of all exploited and oppressed people could only succeed in close alliance with the Soviet Union.[29]

The German authorities monitoring the communist movement noted that, as the anniversary approached, the party organ *Rote Fahne* reported on an almost daily basis on the Soviet Union. Although many of the articles dealt with the historic events of the Russian revolution, it was commented that these were only partially meant as history lessons for the German workers, and also had the object of teaching important lessons on how to realise the revolution in Germany.[30]

By 27 April 1927, the IAH had managed to secure the support of over 200 intellectuals, who joined in a 'German Committee for the Celebration of the Ten Year Anniversary of Soviet Russia'. Among the names were the Jewish German physician and sexologist Magnus Hirschfeld, the visual artist Heinrich Zille, the author and playwright Alfons Paquet, the revolutionary socialist Kurt Hiller, the chairman of the German IAH Alfons Goldschmidt, and the author and journalist Kurt Tucholsky, soon to be famous for his satiric book *Deutschland, Deutschland über alles*.[31] The gathering in this way of intellectual supporters and sympathisers provided the campaign with a sense of importance and a legitimacy that went far beyond the circles and issues of the communist party, and which constituted a first step in the shaping of the campaign into a broad event.

ORGANISING DELEGATIONS OF FRIENDS AND COMRADES

The invitation of the delegates to the Moscow celebrations was decided upon slowly. Sending workers' delegations to Soviet Russia was already an established practice, but the organisation of larger versions, combined with the celebrations of the October Revolution, was new.[32] Moreover, in earlier years, workers' delegations had been sent from Britain and Germany, but they had never been invited to Moscow at the same time. This posed a central technical and organisational challenge for the preparations. However, Münzenberg was convinced that this would definitely pay off, with greater interest in the delegations, and more reports in the communist and left-wing press internationally. To receive the delegations one after the other would not have the same spectacular effect as receiving them all at the same time; and the effect would be much stronger if they managed to bring together, for example, trade union members from Britain, India, and South Africa, to unite in a symbolic demonstration in Moscow. Münzenberg even envisaged it as an event similar to the anti-imperialist congress in Brussels, but this time assembled in solidarity with the Soviet Union. At this point, it was still intended that the delegations would visit Moscow between 15 September and 15 October so that they could then participate in their home countries as witnesses returning from the land of October – though this later changed. All delegations were to be invited by their Russian equivalent: for example the major group of around 500 trade unionists was to be invited by the Russian trade unions, and co-operators similarly by the Russian co-operators, and scientists by the Russian academy. All in all, 200 delegates from the Comintern's international 'non-party mass organisations' (also described as above-party organisations) like the IAH or the International Red Aid (MOPR), were to be invited.[33]

It was planned that the IAH would send twenty-five delegates from its various national sections. The LAI was to invite thirty European delegates and 100 delegates of the league's colonial and semi-colonial members. However, due to the close interconnection between the various international communist-led committees and sympathising organisations, specific lists of names had to be compiled so that one person did not by mistake receive an invitation from several organisations.[34] All in all, the Comintern approved of receiving 1000 foreign delegates; from Germany there were in total 173 delegates sent to the Soviet Union. Significantly, delegations were not all organised on a national basis. There was not one big German delegation, but a multitude of international delegations of the different sympathising organisations. Although many of the delegates were communists, the conference of the 'Friends of the Soviet Union' in particular brought together ordinary workers who were not communists. These were invited for a fourteen-day trip during which they travelled across the country to see socialism in construction and to meet the Soviet people.[35]

In total, there were three German workers' delegations sent to Moscow for the celebrations, comprising eighty-four worker delegates in all. As part of the plan to send the delegates, a fundraising campaign and a collection of signatures and greetings to the Soviet Union was undertaken. The target of the campaign had been 300,000 signatures, but the final count was slightly lower and 250,000 signed the solidarity address called 'Die Einheit' (Unity). There was also a fundraising drive that collected 25,000 German marks reserved for the financing of travel to the Soviet Union and support of delegates' families while they were abroad.[36]

The IAH delegation departed from Berlin on 17 October, and arrived in Moscow two days later. Münzenberg and the Italian communist Francesco Misiano were joined by six Germans, three French people, two Czech people, two Dutch people, two Britons, a representative from the Balkans, and a member of the German workers' photography movement. They were invited by the Russian bureau of the IAH in Moscow to a small conference dealing with the history of the IAH in Russia, there known as the *Mezhrabpom*.[37] The program of the IAH delegation in Moscow included sightseeing, visits to the factories, a visit to the Museum of the Revolution, a look at the IAH's film studio called *Mezhrabpom-Film*, and a visit to a Moscow prison to inspect the conditions of the prisoners. Moreover a trip to Krim was planned. After these tours, in contrast to the previous plan, the delegation was set to participate in the major celebrations in Moscow.[38]

All of the IAH's twenty-eight delegates from Germany were to be present in Moscow no later than 5 November, so that they could join the grand celebrations. Contrary to earlier German delegations to Moscow, this time the Germans were actively involved in the parades, festive meetings, and the international Congress of Friends. In Leningrad, the delegation was invited to a jubilee conference of the Soviet Union's Central Executive Committee where the 'Manifesto of the ten year anniversary of the revolution' was proclaimed. According to a report by German security services, this made an impression on the delegates, not least due to its enthusiastic reception by the Leningrad workers, and several of the delegates were invited to the rostrum to bear witness to their 'powerful demonstration' of support. Similarly in Moscow, the delegates witnessed the parade of the Red Army, the armed march of the Moscow factory battalion [*Betriebsbataillione*], and the youth and women's battalions. The report concluded that witnessing such powerful demonstrations by armed proletarian masses must have worked as the best possible propaganda for the world revolution.[39] Again, the celebrations in Moscow were constructed into an extravagant experience. There the delegates were ordinary workers, part of a transnational workers' community celebrating the creation and growing strength of the first workers' state.

At the conference of the Friends of the Soviet Union, the Soviet premier Alexei Rykov had spoken on behalf of the Soviet government on the country's ten years of socialist construction. However, the main item in the congress programme was the issue of the 'USSR and the war danger'. Bukharin gave a speech on the campaigns of the Comintern followed by a group representing the world's communist parties presenting a resolution on the activities of the opposition in the Russian party. In this resolution, they expressed their fullest sympathy with the party in its fight against Trotsky. Ominously, already at the October celebration there was a public declaration of the importance of fighting the 'Enemies of the October Revolution' which was signed by the representatives of the communist parties. The conference in Moscow resulted in the publication of various manifestoes. The principal one was entitled 'Against Imperialist War! For the Soviet Union! For revolutionary China!'[40]

The celebrations in Moscow were clouded by the perceived rising threat of an imperialist war. Barbusse argued in his speech at the Congress of Friends that the external threat to the young socialist republic was indeed real. Already at the first demonstration inaugurating the jubilee celebrations in Moscow, the People's Commissar for War, Kliment Voroshilov, had declared that 'during the past decade the Russian proletariat had to fight before constructing and that in the coming decades it will be probably compelled to fight before continuing to reconstruct'. Thus, according to Barbusse, it was the duty of the assembled delegations from around the world to spread the word about the Soviet Union's accomplishments and demand an active international defence of the USSR.[41] The commemorations of the revolution strove to attest the significance of the Soviet Union for the workers of the world, and to highlight the importance and reality of the transnational community of the workers. The Soviet Union was an unknown foreign territory, but the celebrations offered a unique chance to forge a lasting impression and new feeling of solidarity towards the USSR.

The 'congress of the 1000' was distinctly different from the congresses of the Communist International that only gathered high ranking communist party delegates together. The congress assembled non-party workers who were free of the usual communist party discipline. *Pravda* declared on 5 November 1927 that this congress was of major significance. It was not only perceived as a way of showcasing the Soviet Union, but presented a unique opportunity to bring together workers from around the world. The perception was that barriers and boundaries constructed between the different races and nationalities by the bourgeoisie and social democrats were a much more severe obstacle for the world revolution than 'all the cannons and bayonets of the bourgeoisie's armies'. However, this revolutionary internationalism was continuously linked with the destiny of the USSR, and the Soviet Union was presented as the fatherland of all exploited classes and oppressed peoples of the entire world.[42]

The congress was not merely a celebration of Russian achievements. For example, the Germans Clara Zetkin and Max Hölz were awarded the 'Order of the Red Banner', which the German communist Robert Siewert accepted on behalf of Hölz, who was still imprisoned in Germany. Siewert declared that they would make it their sacred duty to inform all workers in Germany that it was time to bring capitalism to its conclusion. Victory, Siewert affirmed, could not be attained through co-operation with capital, but through a hard and cruel fight. He concluded his speech by declaring in Russian 'Long live the Red Army! Long live the world revolution!'[43] When the congress concluded, *Pravda* proclaimed on 13 November that it was the clearest proof that the message of the 'Great October Revolution' had spread widely beyond the borders of the Soviet Union, and it moreover gave hope to all those workers whose views were suppressed in the social democratic parties and reformist Amsterdam International.[44]

After the public celebrations in Moscow, the programme continued with several conferences that actively involved the IAH's delegation: a youth conference of the friends of the Soviet Union, the international conference of revolutionary writers, the conference of the executive committee of the peasant international (Krestintern), a plenum of the executive committee of the Sport International (Sportintern), a conference of the MOPR, the second all-Russian conference of women workers and peasants, a meeting of the miners' international propaganda committee, and a conference of workers' correspondents. Besides these meetings, several of the German delegates had visited a propaganda school for miners, a conference of the Comintern's military section, politburo meetings of the Comintern and Profintern, and Comintern propaganda courses. Several of these delegates were also invited to meet Stalin.[45]

Symbolically, when it was time to leave Moscow the three German workers' delegations presented a declaration to the

Moscow workers, addressed to all Soviet workers and to the Red Army. This was signed by sixty-five of the German delegates, who pledged to engage in the defence of the Soviet Union and its work of socialist construction. Apparently the trip had been a huge success in the effort to promote a more sympathetic view of the USSR among non-communists. The delegation had numbered eighty-four in total, meaning that only nineteen delegates had declined to sign the declaration. Once back in Germany, the social-democratic delegates wrote an open letter to the SPD describing what they had witnessed during their travels. This report was much celebrated in the communist press, as the delegates declared that the SPD press had fabricated lies about the realities of life in the Soviet Union.

Significantly for the IAH's delegation, the visit was directly linked to the workers' famine relief organised for Soviet Russia by Münzenberg and the IAH between 1921 and 1923. It was argued that the aim of the 1927 visit had been to strengthen the existing transnational bond of solidarity between the IAH and the Soviet Union, and that the ultimate aim of sending delegates to the Soviet Union was that they should, on their return, engage even more strongly in the campaign against an imperialist war of aggression on the Soviet Union.[46] In a sense, their participation in the celebrations provided an answer to the question: why should the workers of Germany or the workers of the world engage in the protection and defence of the Soviet Union? For if the October Revolution was worth celebrating, it was definitely also worth defending.

ENTANGLED CELEBRATIONS? BRINGING THE MESSAGE OF OCTOBER TO GERMANY

When the worker delegations returned to Germany, they performed another symbolic act of transnational solidarity. Russian banners from large factories in Moscow had been sent with the delegation to Germany and, according to a report by the German authorities, the workers at a Krupp and Thyssen factory had been presented with them.[47]

With a distinct sense of concern, the German security services concluded that the trip to the Soviet Union had stirred the workers, not only to support the Soviet Union against the war danger, but to support more strongly the world revolution and efforts to form a workers' united front. In this spirit, a representative of the workers' Esperanto movement had published a travel account which described the USSR as a fortress of the world proletariat where socialism was actually being constructed. It was hence their duty to build a dam against all malicious attacks and lies against the Soviet Union and while truly defending this fortress to prepare for the world revolution. The revolution's tenth anniversary was here understood as an incentive to work even more intensely for the spread and empowerment of the red front.[48] It would seem that Münzenberg's plans had in many ways had the anticipated outcome.

When the delegates returned to Germany, many were active in reporting their impressions as witnesses of the Soviet Union's achievements. In mid-December 1927, it was estimated that members of the German IAH delegation made a total of sixty appearances at meetings and rallies. Moreover, that same month, the IAH's so-called 'delegation of intellectuals' organised a major meeting in Berlin to report on the anniversary celebrations.[49] One of the first opportunities to give these reports was the IAH's fourth international congress organised in Berlin, 20-22 November 1927, which Max Hodann addressed on behalf of the delegation. According to a police report, the conference was attended by representatives from Russia, France, Czechoslovakia, Britain, Belgium, Italy, Sweden, the Netherlands, 'Africa', and the USA. In this way, the echoes of the celebrations were carried even further, through the transnational networks of organisations like the IAH. On this note, Münzenberg at the conference urged all the world's workers to use every accessible means of mobilising the working masses against the preparations that were taking place for war against the Soviet Union.[50]

Hodann in reporting to the conference stated that what had made the strongest impression on him was the Soviet Union's ability to mobilise and activate the masses. This, he maintained, was perhaps the best defence against those critics of the USSR who falsely believed that it was a dictatorship run by a small clique of communists employing the brutal methods of the Cheka. Moreover, Hodann highlighted how, despite the burden of the legacies of tsarism, war, hunger, and civil war, this had not hindered the Soviet Union from undertaking vast construction works. The socialist society had not yet been achieved, but this, Hodann noted, was an impossibility after only five years of reconstruction. To secure continuing socialist construction, Hodann urged that each should make it their personal responsibility to convince all workers in the capitalist countries that it was their duty to hinder the commencement of an anti-Soviet war. Hodann further described the unforgettable impression made by the Soviet Union's firm belief in international solidarity. There was, he elaborated, no longer any question of which nationality one belonged to; whether you were a German, Briton, French, Russian, or Chinese was insignificant, and what alone mattered was whether you were 'white or red'. Then, one was among brothers, and, in the spirit of international solidarity, Hodann explained that it was the duty of workers the world over to secure the construction of socialism in the Soviet Union. It was thus immensely important that they make it clear to all capitalist countries that, wherever a war against the Soviet Union was commenced, the international proletariat would make sure of transforming it into a civil war against their own governments.[51]

In addition to congresses and rallies in Germany, the anniversary received a great deal of attention in the IAH's press and especially the *AIZ*, which was published weekly with a print run of between 220,000 and 300,000 copies. The magazine used effective visual strategies with the aim of nurturing the bonds of solidarity between the workers of the world and the Soviet Union. In its special issue on the anniversary, it included statements by prominent Soviet leaders as well as by sympathetic intellectuals from Germany itself. The artist Käthe Kollwitz remarked in her statement that, although she was not a communist, she still appreciated the historical meaning of a revolution that, according to her, could only be compared to the French Revolution. Edo Fimmen, general secretary of the International Transport Workers' Federation, maintained in his *AIZ* statement that one either stood with the Soviet Union, or was against it. There was no middle position, and if you were against it, you were wittingly or unwittingly a supporter of reaction and the counter-revolution. In another statement printed in the *AIZ*, the Soviet president Mikhail Kalinin lambasted all critics of the USSR and highlighted that what once had only been a dream was now being realised in practice by millions of workers and peasants in the Soviet Union. Sergei Eisenstein meanwhile described it as simply ten years of the impossible and unimaginable.[52]

The entangled celebrations between the USSR and Germany were clearly visible in the *AIZ*. Although only a limited number of delegates could be sent to Moscow, through photos the illustrated press offered a new way to participate in the faraway spectacle. Images of the IAH delegation's enthusiastic arrival at the Moscow railway station were placed side-by-side with an image of an equally enthusiastic crowd of Russian workers who had come to greet the foreign delegates. This portrayed a classic image of 'proletarian internationalism' where comrades from all around the globe were united for a common cause: the world revolution. Contrary to typical state jubilees, the main representatives of foreign countries were not diplomats or heads of government, but ordinary workers and intellectuals, who were received and celebrated as honoured guests. In 1927, this seems to have still been possible before the Soviet authorities began to perceive foreigners increasingly as strangers or potential enemies and spies.[53]

According to the figures which Münzenberg reported to Moscow, the twenty-page jubilee issue of the *AIZ* was printed in 350,000 copies. Moreover, there was a major book project *Illustrierte Geschichte der russischen Revolution* (*Illustrated History of the Russian Revolution*) that was published, with a print run of 30,000 copies, initially in a series of twenty-four booklets, and then as single volumes in German, English, Russian, and Swedish. Another important publication was a thousand-page guidebook on the Soviet Union entitled *Führer durch Sowjetrussland* and published in English and French as well as German.[54] All of these efforts helped to internationalise the commemorations and celebrations of October within the transnational civil society.

Parallel to the sending of delegations to witness the October celebrations in Moscow, the cultural achievements of the Soviet Union were put on display in Germany. In March 1927, Münzenberg had suggested to the Comintern secretariat that the Comintern's Agitprop Department assist him in organising a number of mass Russian cultural events and celebrations in Europe. Münzenberg specifically asked for the theatre group called the Blue Shirts to be sent on a tour to Germany.[55] This was organised by the IAH with the aim of spreading sympathy for the USSR amongst the wider population, and it has subsequently been described as a major factor in the establishment of a wave of new agitprop troupes in Germany. In total, the Blue Shirts performed in twenty-five cities to about 150,000 spectators, and in this way created unique spectacles for purposes of international solidarity and the extended celebration of the Soviet Union.[56]

CONCLUSIONS

One could argue that the celebrations in Moscow in 1927 made a major contribution to the Soviet Union's global image as the fatherland of all oppressed and exploited. The campaign as conceived by Münzenberg was, on the one hand, based on the need to showcase the economic, cultural, and political achievements of the young socialist republic. This was important in the global struggle against the Soviet Union's critics and adversaries in demonstrating that something revolutionary was indeed in the making. On the other hand, this was also the opportunity to enhance the image of the Soviet Union as a part of the transnational workers' community. It was not only a Russian revolution that was being celebrated, but the very idea of a world revolution, of a social revolution that could conclusively alter human history. Conversely, by showing that the Soviet Union really was a beacon of light, it made it easier to argue that the workers of the world should participate in its defence.

The transnational interaction took place at different levels. First, there was the transnational organisational level, where a number of leaders of international communist organisations interacted in the co-ordination of the celebrations. Secondly, there was the level of civil society, as German workers and delegates travelled to Moscow to witness at first hand what for most of them had, until then, remained a foreign land of the unknown. This brought to life a completely new level of transnational interconnectedness between Germany and the people of the USSR. In their capacity as witnesses, the delegates could then return home to take the message to others and speak with a different kind of authenticity. Thirdly, the publicity surrounding the event was greatly enhanced, as the IAH's illustrated newspapers depicted the events in Moscow and re-created the transnational encounters for a broader German public. The final form of transnational interaction occurred in the cultural sphere, as Soviet culture was imported into Germany, though the Blue Shirts' tour, which inspired a broad movement of agitprop theatres around the country. The echoes of the commemorations were thus transmitted through a vivid network that moved in both directions between civil society actors, cultural figures, and newspapers in Germany on the one hand, and the Soviet Union on the other. In the process, a distinct new organisation was created, in the form of the Soviet Friendship Societies.

Although the October celebrations were based on an idea of equality within the transnational community of workers, the events in Moscow also illustrated the rising dominance of the Russians. The 'fatherland' of all workers wanted the world to celebrate its achievements, and was empowered by the presence of the international delegations and revolutionary figures who pledged to defend the USSR. Within the context of the time, the commemorations represented a unique spectacle of international solidarity, but at the same time they also marked a turn in the common understanding of international solidarity, towards a new form of unconditional and uncritical loyalty to the Soviet Union.

NOTES

1. Henry Barbusse, 'Report at the congress of the friends of the Soviet Union on 10 November 1927, on the danger of an imperialist war against the Soviet Union', RGASPI, f. 495, op. 30, d. 357, ll. 3-11, here l. 3. See also forthcoming volume/articles by Jean-François Fayet.
2. Barbusse, RGASPI, f. 495, op. 30, d. 357, ll. 3-11, here ll. 3-5.
3. Michael David-Fox, *Showcasing the Great Experiment. Cultural Diplomacy and Western Visitors to the Soviet Union, 1921-1941*, Oxford University Press: Oxford, 2012. For 1927, see especially pp122-127. For Switzerland, see the detailed study by Jean-François Fayet, *VOKS*.

Le laboratoire helvétique. Histoire de la diplomatie culturelle soviétique durant l'entre-deux-guerres, Georg: Chêne-Bourg, 2014. See also Ludmila Stern, *Western Intellectuals and the Soviet Union, 1920-40. From Red Square to the Left Bank*, Routledge: London, 2009.
4. See further on the IAH's solidarity campaigns in Kasper Braskén, *The International Workers' Relief, Communism, and Transnational Solidarity. Willi Münzenberg in Weimar Germany*, Palgrave Macmillan: Houndmills, 2015. On the previous research on Münzenberg, see Bernhard H. Bayerlein, Kasper Braskén, Uwe Sonnenberg and Gleb J. Albert, 'Research on Willi Münzenberg (1889-1940). Life, activities and solidarity networks. A bibliography', *International Newsletter of Communist Studies*, Vol. 18 No. 25, 2012, pp104-122.
5. For a discussion on the Comintern's transnational above-party organisations, see Holger Weiss (ed.), *International Communism and Transnational Solidarity. Radical Networks, Mass Movements and Global Politics, 1919-1939*, Brill: Leiden, 2016. For Germany, see the classic study by Hartmann Wunderer, *Arbeitervereine und Arbeiterparteien. Kultur- und Massenorganisationen in der Arbeiterbewegung (1890-1933)*, Campus Verlag: Frankfurt/New York, 1980.
6. Mauno Heimo to Münzenberg, 8 January 1927, RGASPI, f. 538, op. 2, d. 40, ll. 12-15; Münzenberg to Heimo, 25 January 1927, RGASPI, f. 538, op. 2, d. 40, l. 50. Heimo was a Finnish high ranking Comintern official.
7. Münzenberg to Heimo, 3 January 1927, RGASPI, f. 538, op. 2, d. 40, ll. 9-10a, here l. 10.
8. Unsigned letter from the Comintern to Münzenberg, 25 January 1927, RGASPI, f. 538, op. 2, d. 40, l. 42.
9. Heimo to Münzenberg, 8 January 1927, RGASPI, f. 538, op. 2, d. 40, ll. 12-15.
10. Münzenberg to Kuusinen, 24 January 1927, RGASPI, f. 538, op. 2, d. 40, ll. 37-41. For an early treatment of the Friendship Societies, see Louis Nemzer, 'The Soviet Friendship Societies', *Public Opinion Quarterly*, Vol. 13 No. 2, 1949, pp265-284.
11. 'Die Gesellschaft der Freunde des neuen Russlands', Niederschrift über die Besprechung des Reichskommissars für Überwachung der öffentlichen Ordnung mit den Nachrichtenstellen der Länder in Berlin, 23-24 January 1925, BArch, R 1507/2050, 1-138, here 101-106.

12. Eduard Fuchs to Clara Zetkin, 27 January 1927; Eduard Fuchs to Olga Kameneva, 27 January 1927; Eduard Fuchs to Olga Kameneva, 31 January 1927, SAPMO-BArch, NY 4005/73, 33-37.
13. Münzenberg to Heimo, 31 January 1927, RGASPI, f. 538, op. 2, d. 40, ll. 65-66.
14. Münzenberg to Bukharin, 1 February 1927, RGASPI, f. 538, op. 2, d. 40, l. 72.
15. Protocol: 'Vorschlag des Gen. Manuilsky betr. Organisierung und Entsendung von Delegationen von der ganzen Welt nach USSR zum 10. Jahrestag der Oktober Revolution und Abhaltung von einem Weltkongress der Werktätigen', Sitzung des Politsekretariats des EKKI, 4 February 1927, RGASPI, f. 495, op. 3, d. 5, ll. 39-50, here l. 39.
16. Sitzung des Politsekretariats des EKKI, 4 February 1927, RGASPI, f. 495, op. 3, d. 5, ll. 39-50, here l. 40.
17. *Ibid.*, here l. 41, ll. 45-46.
18. Unsigned letter from the Comintern to Münzenberg, 4 February 1927, RGASPI, f. 538, op. 2, d. 40, l. 76.
19. Unsigned letter from the Comintern to Münzenberg, 9 February 1927, RGASPI, f. 538, op. 2, d. 40, ll. 107-109.
20. On the LAI, see further the work of Fredrik Petersson, *'We are Neither Visionaries Nor Utopian Dreamers'. Willi Münzenberg, the League against Imperialism and the Comintern, 1925-1933*, Edwin Mellen Press: Lewiston, 2014.
21. Unsigned letter from the Comintern to Münzenberg, 19 March 1927, RGASPI, f. 538, op. 2, d. 40, l. 160.
22. Münzenberg to the Secretariat of the Comintern, 'Bericht über den Stand der Aktion "10-Jahre Sowjetrussland"', 26 March 1927, RGASPI, f. 538, op. 2, d. 40, ll. 169-176, here l. 169.
23. Münzenberg to the Secretariat of the Comintern, RGASPI, f. 538, op. 2, d. 40, ll. 169-176.
24. Münzenberg to Heimo, 25 January 1927, RGASPI, f. 538, op. 2, d. 40, l. 50.
25. Heimo to Münzenberg, 8 January 1927, RGASPI, f. 538, op. 2, d. 40, ll. 12-15.
26. Münzenberg to Heimo, 31 January 1927, RGASPI, f. 538, op. 2, d. 40, ll. 65-66.
27. Münzenberg to Kuusinen, 1 February 1927, RGASPI, f. 538, op. 2, d. 40, ll. 68-69.

28. Unsigned letter from Moscow to the Secretariat of the EKKI (copy also to the CC of the KPD), 12 April 1927, RGASPI, f. 495, op. 18, d. 571, ll. 37-38; Unsigned letter to Secretariat of the ECCI (Copy to the CC of the KPD), 22 April 1927, SAPMO-BArch, RY 5/I 6/10/30, 23-24.
29. Plan für die Kampagne: 10 Jahre Sowjetunion, RGASPI, f. 495, op. 60, d. 117, ll. 69-75, here ll. 69-70.
30. Die kommunistische Kampagne 'Zehn Jahre Sowjet-Russland', R.Ko.In.Nr.122, 15 July 1927, BArch, R 1507/2034, 39.
31. Münzenberg to Piatnitzki, 27 April 1927, RGASPI, f. 538, op. 2, d. 40, ll. 236-237.
32. See for example the published report on a German workers' delegation: *Was sahen 58 deutsche Arbeiter in Russland? Bericht der deutschen Arbeiter-Delegation über ihren Aufenthalt in Rußland vom 14. Juli bis zum 28. August 1925*, Neuer Deutscher Verlag: Berlin, 1925.
33. Bericht des Gen. Münzenberg über die vorbereitende Kommission anlässlich des 10-Jahrestag des Oktoberrevolutions, closed meeting in Moscow, 25 May 1927, RGASPI, f. 495, op. 60, d. 117, ll. 36-40, here ll. 37-39.
34. Unsigned letter from the Comintern to Münzenberg, 22 July 1927, RGASPI, f. 538, op. 2, d. 40, ll. 292-293.
35. German security services report, 'Die internationalen Kongresse in Moskau anlässlich der Feier des 10. Jahrestages der russischen Revolution unter Teilnahme deutscher Delegierter', 24 December 1927, BArch, R 1507/1050d, 100-102.
36. German security services report, 'R.Ko.In.124, Berlin, 24 Dezember 1927', BArch, R 1507/2037, 12.
37. The names of the IAH's German delegation were Ernst Grau (Essen, secretary of the IAH in the Ruhr District); Johannes Höcker (Halle, IAH-secretary in Halle-Merseburg); Erich Schumann (Dresden, secretary of the IAH in the Dresden-district); Eugen Heilig (workers' photographer); Max Hodann (Berlin, second chairman of the German IAH); Rudolf Teichmüller (IAH Ruhla); Hans Wasewitz (Berlin, secretary of the IAH-district of Berlin-Brandenburg). Münzenberg to Kuusinen, 17 October 1927, RGASPI, f. 495, op. 30, d. 392, ll. 93-95. Münzenberg to Heimo, 3 October 1927, RGASPI, f. 538, op. 2, d. 40, l. 325. Die deutschen Arbeiterdelegationen in Sowjetrussland anlässlich der Feier des 10. Jahrestages der Russischen Revolution, BArch, R 1507/2037, 17-22, here 18.

38. 'IAH-Delegation nach Rußland', *Mahnruf*, No. 11, October 1927; 'Die IAH-Delegation berichtet. Die Behandlung der Gefangenen in Deutschland und in Rußland', *Mahnruf*, No. 14, 15 November 1927; Hans Wasewitz, 'Bericht von der Besichtigung der Gummifabrik "Krasny Bogatyr" durch die IAH-Delegation', *Mahnruf*, No. 15, 1 December 1927.
39. German security services report, 'R.Ko.In.124, Berlin, 24 Dezember 1927', BArch, R 1507/2037, 18-19.
40. German security services report, 'Die internationalen Kongresse in Moskau anlässlich der Feier des 10. Jahrestages der russischen Revolution unter Teilnahme deutscher Delegierter', 24 December 1927, BArch, R 1507/1050d, 100-102.
41. Barbusse, RGASPI, f. 495, op. 30, d. 357, ll. 3-11, here ll. 6-11.
42. Die internationalen Kongresse in Moskau, 24 December 1927, BArch, R 1507/1050d, 100-102.
43. Die internationalen Kongresse in Moskau, 24 December 1927, BArch, R 1507/1050d, 102-102a.
44. Die internationalen Kongresse in Moskau, 24 December 1927, BArch, R 1507/1050d, 102a.
45. German security services report, 'R.Ko.In.124, Berlin, 24 Dezember 1927', BArch, R 1507/2037, 19-20.
46. 'IAH-Delegation nach Rußland', *Mahnruf*, No. 11, October 1927; 'Die IAH-Delegation berichtet. Die Behandlung der Gefangenen in Deutschland und in Rußland', *Mahnruf*, No. 14, 15 November 1927; Hans Wasewitz, 'Bericht von der Besichtigung der Gummifabrik "Krasny Bogatyr" durch die IAH-Delegation', *Mahnruf*, No. 15, 1 December 1927.
47. German security services report, 'R.Ko.In.124, Berlin, 24 Dezember 1927', BArch, R 1507/2037, 20-21.
48. German security services report, 'R.Ko.In.124, Berlin, 24 Dezember 1927', BArch, R 1507/2037, 21-22.
49. Francesco Misiano to Heimo, 12 December 1927, RGASPI, f. 538, op. 3, d. 92, ll. 51-52.
50. Der 4. internationale Kongress der IAH, BArch, R 1507/1050d, 98-99.
51. Protocol from the IAH's conference in Berlin, 20-22 November 1927. Transcript of speech by Max Hodann, RGASPI, f. 538, op. 1, d. 7, ll. 31-37.
52. 'Zehn Jahre Soziale Revolution', *AIZ*, No. 43, 26 October 1927.

53. Brigitte Studer, *The Transnational World of the Cominternians*, Palgrave Macmillan: Houndmills, 2015, pp126-135.
54. Münzenberg to Heimo, 18 October 1927, RGASPI, f. 538, op. 2, d. 40, l. 331.
55. Münzenberg to Heimo, 11 October 1927, RGASPI, f. 538, op. 2, d. 40, l. 328; Münzenberg to the Secretariat of the Comintern, 'Bericht über den Stand der Aktion "10-Jahre Sowjetrussland"', 26 March 1927, RGASPI, f. 538, op. 2, d. 40, ll. 169-176.
56. See further in Braskén, *op. cit.*, pp178-181.

Exporting Soviet Commemoration: The Spanish Civil War and the October Revolution, 1936-1939

Daniel Kowalsky

INTRODUCTION

Despite the diverse range of commemorations marking the October Revolution of 1917 – in Red Square, across the Soviet Republics and beyond – no setting could compete with the unique circumstances of the Spanish Republic during the civil war of 1936-1939. The internationalisation of the war, from its beginning, created an improbable scenario in which the Soviet Union soon became the principal supplier of weaponry to the besieged democratic government in Madrid. The Kremlin's commitment to the Republic, continuing until the end of the war, was multi-faceted, and included the dispatch and deployment of modern aircraft and armour, military advisors, and technicians, but also support for an international volunteer army, recruited from national communist cells. The International Brigades, together with the dispatch of Soviet hardware, gave the Republic early respite from the nationalist assault on Madrid. Yet it also presented Moscow with an irresistible opportunity to exploit a captive audience reliant on Soviet assistance. Soviet propaganda of every variety, from print culture to the cinema, flooded the Republic. A most curious export was the Bolsheviks' inimitable secular celebration calendar. In due course, the Spanish Civil War would become the backdrop for some of the most elaborately staged October jubilees outside the Soviet Union.

That no foreign country in the late 1930s marked the October Revolution's anniversaries with the same enthusiasm as the Spanish Republic was improbable to say the least. Prior to 1936, Spain had never figured prominently in the Russian imagination. Before the revolution, the two imperial crowns had maintained diplomatic relations, but economically, militarily and culturally, the destinies of the Slavic and Spanish peoples rarely overlapped. True, the distinctive Spanish musical idiom had provided some inspiration to nineteenth century Russian composers, for example, Glinka's 1848 'A Night in Madrid' and Rimsky-Korsakov's 1887 'Capriccio Espagnol'.[1] Similarly, in the late nineteenth century, Spanish translations of the novels of Gogol, Tolstoy, and Dostoyevsky enjoyed wide popularity throughout Spain.[2] But geography, and then ideology, kept these two towering cultures largely ignorant of one another.

After the Bolsheviks came to power, the Spanish government of Alfonso XIII withdrew its ambassador from St Petersburg, refusing all overtures from the new regime. In response to its poor reception on the Iberian Peninsula, the Soviet leadership delayed establishing more than a token Comintern presence in Spain, and proved themselves as uninterested in Spain as their tsarist forbears. That Castilian, despite its hundreds of millions of native speakers, was never elevated to a Comintern language, suggests that Moscow saw scant potential for revolutionary ferment in either Spain or its former colonies in Central or South America. It says much that, in the mid-1930s, there was no Spanish-Russian, nor Russian-Spanish dictionary in print in either state, nor anywhere in the world.[3]

The Comintern downplayed the promise of the Iberian left, but in Spain, revolutionary parties were encouraged by the

Bolshevik Revolution. Initially, the Barcelona anarchists were euphoric, and interpreted Lenin's coup as an anarchist event, but six months later, the anarchist trade union *Confederación Nacional del Trabajo* (National Confederation of Labour or CNT) was more restrained.[4] For their part, the *Partido Socialista Obrero de España* (Spanish Socialist Workers Party) and its trade union, the *Unión General del Trabajo* (The General Union of Labour or PSOE/UGT), commemorated with enthusiasm the first jubilee in November 1918.[5] Expressions of overt sympathies for the revolution reached their apex in the so-called '*Trienio Bolschevista*' of 1918-1920, a three-year period of labour unrest and strike waves during which the Soviet experiment was frequently exalted.

Across the decade of the 1920s and into the early 1930s, Spain's left-wing parties and intellectuals were increasingly fascinated by the Soviet Union. The economic, social and cultural advances of the Bolsheviks, together with the crises of the capitalist west and the rise of national socialism, led not a few Spaniards to see the USSR in utopian terms. Political tourism to the Soviet Union, and resultant published travelogues, were soon in vogue among Spanish writers, artists, and poets. If few Spaniards attended the 1927 Moscow jubilee, the broadly disseminated propaganda around that event led to deeper cultural ties between the two countries.[6] With the coming of the Second Republic in April 1931, this soon extended to the diplomatic sphere; by summer 1933, Spain had formally recognised the legality of the USSR.[7]

The Spanish Civil War, which began on 18-19 July 1936, presented Moscow with a dilemma. Since 1917, the Bolsheviks had encouraged revolution and civil war among the communist faithful. Now revolution and civil war had broken out in Spain, but, for the party, 1936 was not 1917. The official Soviet strategy was cooperation with non-revolutionary parties in Europe against the common threat of fascism.[8] In Spain, the onset of hostilities led to a power vacuum in the centre, which was quickly filled by revolutionary parties. The popular revolution, centred in large cities still under Republican control, undertook property redistribution and widespread collectivisation. Critically, that revolutionary fervour also supplied people and enthusiasm in the first pitched battles with the nationalists.

For the Kremlin, it was never clear how Soviet aid to the Republic would not appear as support for revolution in Spain, and consequently Stalin responded with extreme caution.[9] Recently declassified documents from the Presidential Archive suggest a Kremlin riveted by the July uprising, but in no hurry to show its hand. Already on 21 July 1936, Comintern official Dimitri Manuilsky had sent Stalin the first update from the field.[10] The following day, the Soviets agreed to sell discounted fuel to Madrid.[11] Then on 23 July, Comintern chief Georgi Dmitrov implored Stalin, in a hand-written note, to issue further orders in response to the evolving situation on the Iberian Peninsula.[12]

The impetus for the Soviet leader to eventually act more forcefully came from numerous quarters.[13] There was the pressure from international communism and the international left, which, from the first days of the war, was mobilised in favour of the Republic. For Moscow to ignore Spain would be to surrender a chance to champion this most popular of causes, and thereby risk alienating the global left. This ideological justification for involvement would have been complemented by the geo-strategic imperative: Spain provided Moscow with an opening not only to confront fascism, but to test both the viability of collective security with western powers and the popular front tactic adopted and made official in 1935 at the Seventh Party Conference. Finally, the financial incentive to the Soviets should not be ignored. The Republic was prepared to pay for foreign military assistance in gold, and the Bank of Spain possessed the fourth largest stocks in the world. For Stalin, what lay in the balance, and what was eventually dispatched to Moscow, was 510 tons of gold valued in 1936 prices at $518 million.[14]

The odd circumstances of the internationalisation of the Spanish Civil War occurred in three phases. First, from late July, the rebels sought and received military support from Nazi Germany and Fascist Italy, catapulting General Francisco Franco into a position of pre-eminence, and allowing the nationalist army to make rapid progress on the march towards Madrid. Second, in early August, the democratic west, led by France and Britain, adopted a position of neutrality, formalised in the Non-Intervention Agreement. That twenty-seven European states signed up to this agreement effectively cut off the Republic from any military assistance.[15] Third and finally, Stalin approved, on 14 September 1936, a substantial military aid package that rescued the Republic from early defeat; the Spanish gold was mobilised on 15 September, one day later.[16]

For Stalin, the war would eventually emerge as an opportunity, but one with many layers. Moscow's military support to the loyalist side occurred in tandem with a propaganda offensive that sought to exploit the captive audience in Republican Spain, and those cultural and ideological imports from the Soviet Union enjoyed an enthusiastic reception. For members of the *Partido Comunista de España* (Communist Party of Spain or PCE) and Comintern front organisations, the arrival of Soviet culture was a long time in coming, and eagerly anticipated. Since the early days of the Republic, the Soviet-Spanish friendship society *Amigos de la Union Soviética* (Friends of the Soviet Union or AUS), had flourished, and had worked closely with Moscow's *Vsesoiuznoe Obshchestvo Kul'turnoi Sviazi s zagranitsei* (All-Union Society for Cultural Relations with Foreign Countries or VOKS).[17] By the end of October 1936, Soviet military aid to the Republic transformed the possibilities for cultural diffusion, and the exchange of ambassadors added key players to a burgeoning project of propaganda. No cultural product was not tried out amongst the populace of Moscow's newfound ally. This would include literature, theatre, music, the plastic arts, poster art, and the cinema. Indeed, the most accessible medium for export to Spain was the cinema, and Soviet film was widely viewed in the wartime Republic, right up its defeat in spring 1939.[18] Then there were the elaborately staged public celebrations of the anniversary of the Bolshevik revolution. Although throughout the entire Soviet period the Kremlin encouraged secular holiday celebrations, the Spanish Civil War coincided with the most frenzied period in the promotion of these public commemorations.[19] During the course of the civil war, Spanish Republicans had the opportunity to celebrate three jubilees: the nineteenth, twentieth, and twenty-first.

THE BATTLE OF MADRID AND THE 1936 JUBILEE OF THE BOLSHEVIK REVOLUTION

The nineteenth anniversary of the October Revolution occurred at a propitious moment in the rapidly evolving relations between Moscow and Madrid. The first Soviet hardware had arrived only on 12 October 1936, barely three weeks before 7 November.[20] In the final days of October, the mobilisation around Madrid of the first Soviet T-26 tanks and I-15 fighters occurred simultaneously with the arrival of the Comintern-sponsored International Brigades.[21] A narrative began to emerge that was picked up and augmented by the loyalist press: nineteen years after the Bolshevik revolution, Soviet arms and communist volunteer fighters, together with the citizens of Madrid, were saving the Spanish capital from counter-revolutionaries. Parallels with the Russian Civil War and the eventual Bolshevik victory over the Whites were made explicit.[22]

As celebrated in the Republic, the jubilee was the first major showcase for a triad that constituted the Soviet propaganda machine on the Iberian Peninsula: VOKS, the Moscow-based supplier;[23] the Soviet diplomatic missions in Madrid and Barcelona, which acted as the coordinators;[24] and the friendship society, AUS, the local distributor. This system was operational by early October 1936, but a dearth of propaganda materials available in the Republic sharply hindered the overall effort and effect. Indeed, the wife of the Barcelona consul, Sofiia Antonov-Ovseenko, lamented on the eve of the jubilee that though the potential for agitation was unlimited, no materials were in place.[25] Only after the first week of November – indeed, at the time of the anniversary itself – did events begin to unfold in a way that favoured increased Soviet cultural involvement in Republican society. It was at this time that the first Soviet military aid was successfully deployed on the Madrid front. The role played by Soviet advisors, tank crews, and pilots in repelling Franco's advance on the capital, rapidly transformed popular attitudes towards the Soviets and greatly contributed to the USSR's growing prestige throughout the Republican zone.[26]

The commemorations marking the nineteenth anniversary were a far cry from those marking the twentieth, yet it could hardly be said that the event passed unnoticed. Towards the end of October 1936, a delegation of Republican workers had left Spain to attend the jubilee in numerous Soviet cities. The delegation was organised and funded by the AUS, although its Soviet itinerary was supplied by Intourist and VOKS, the invitation to attend having come from the Soviet syndicates.[27] In Spain, the group's departure was treated with much fanfare, and touted by the communist daily *Mundo Obrero* as an indication of the rising level of Soviet-Republican solidarity.[28] The delegation's subsequent participation in the Soviet festivities received extensive coverage in communist and left-wing newspapers.[29] A surviving

Soviet newsreel of this event gives some sense of the privileged status enjoyed by the Spaniards in the Red Square festivities.[30] In Republican cities, the AUS organised public gatherings marking the revolution. In Bilbao, the regional government granted the local AUS chapter permission to hold a 7 November rally in the city's largest meeting hall, the Coliseo de Albia.[31] The event, however, was poorly attended, as many of the invited groups declined to participate.[32] The AUS was more successful at screening Soviet films in conjunction with the anniversary.[33] These included a gala showing in Madrid's Cine Monumental of a hagiographic treatment of Lenin entitled 'Genius of the Revolution'.[34] Nor were commemorations limited solely to the AUS and their followers. The Socialist UGT organised a public rally celebrating the October Revolution.[35] The leftist press drew explicit parallels between the Soviet example and events unfolding in Spain: 'In history, November 7, 1917 marks the triumph of the Russian Revolution; November 7, 1936 will become the date marking the victory of our forces'.[36]

MAY DAY AND OTHER SOVIET HOLIDAYS IN THE REPUBLICAN ZONE

Between the nineteenth and twenty-first anniversaries of the Russian Revolution, the Republic's pro-Soviet sympathisers and their Moscow contacts endeavoured to convert other Soviet holidays and commemorations into events worthy of mass mobilisation in Republican Spain. For May 1937, the AUS organised a national lottery to select a group of workers who would represent Spain in the festivities in Moscow.[37] After receiving a rousing send-off, the group steamed to Odessa aboard a Soviet ship, the *Feliks Dzerzhinskii*.[38] In a pattern by then typical of coverage of Spanish delegations in the USSR, the Republican press breathlessly followed their month-long itinerary through Soviet cities, factories, collective farms, and cultural institutions.[39] As one might expect, the Soviet press also gave substantial coverage to the Spanish visitors, stressing above all the delegation's supplication before Stalin at the Moscow May Day parade, an event duly recorded by *Soyuzkino*'s newsreel teams.[40] Back in Spain, May Day was fêted with extensive references to all things Soviet, with the usual variety of propaganda marshalled to the cause.[41] May Day 1938 was treated in much the same fashion, with wide Republican press coverage of the celebrations occurring in the Soviet Union and the dispatch of Spanish delegates.[42]

When the Spanish delegation to May Day 1937 finally returned from the USSR in early June, the AUS put them to use in propaganda events celebrating Soviet society.[43] At conferences, lectures, and rallies, the delegates spoke in hyperbolic terms of the glories they had witnessed in the USSR. Said one, 'I have returned with a magnificent impression'.[44] At Barcelona's Ateneo Popular, one recent returnee presented a series of six talks on different issues concerning the USSR, including: economic life, the rural question, social life, the family in the USSR, maternity and infant care, and the problem of prostitution in the USSR.[45] In the August issue of the AUS's own publication, *Rusia de Hoy,* a two-page spread provided an overview of the delegates' visit, and included several pictures of the Spaniards interacting happily with Soviet citizens and members of the government.[46] To support augmented interest, the AUS stepped up its attempts to disseminate a wide variety of propaganda materials. On the Plaça de Catalunya, the busy pedestrian circle in the centre of Barcelona, the local AUS chapter erected a literature stand where pamphlets, books, and other small items were sold to the public.[47]

The propaganda activities that followed May Day were not the first in which AUS recruited returning delegates to muster support for their cause. To a lesser degree, delegates returning from the nineteenth anniversary visit had also been employed in this way. Indeed, incorporation of these worker eyewitnesses into pro-Soviet campaigns was part of VOKS's strategy in the Republic. In an October 1936 letter to VOKS, Sofiia Antonov-Ovseenko indicated that returning delegates would enhance the propaganda program being implemented by the Barcelona consulate. 'We plan on making broad use of their statements', the consul's wife wrote.[48] Thereafter, the post-tour speaking engagements and appearances became a standard feature of all five major delegations from the Republic to the USSR. These events were always carefully monitored by high-ranking Soviet officials present in Spain, who reported the reactions back to Moscow.[49] More to the point, care was taken to ensure that propaganda focused on the achievements of the USSR since October 1917, rather than the revolution itself. This was the case for Republican commemorations on 7 November and 1 May, but also during observations of other Soviet holidays appropriated by Moscow's Republican allies: International Women's Day,[50] the Pushkin Jubilee,[51] the anniversary of the founding of the Comintern,[52] the anniversary of the Red Army,[53] and Lenin Day,[54] which commemorated the revolutionary's death on 23 January.

THE TWENTIETH ANNIVERSARY COMMEMORATIONS

The appropriation of Soviet holidays for the Republic's calendar continued apace after the limited successes of the nineteenth anniversary and May Day 1937. To ensure a wider audience for the jubilee in November 1937, VOKS and its allies in the Republic made every effort to publicise the event more fully. On 25 May 1937, VOKS wrote to the Valencia-based *Asociación Española de Relaciones Culturales con la Unión Soviética* (Spanish Association for Cultural Relations with the Soviet Union or AERCU) outlining a tentative schedule of activities for the jubilee. 'We think it appropriate to make arrangement for the widest possible variety of happenings related to the twentieth anniversary', VOKS declared. 'This should include, but need not be limited to, soirées, concerts, expositions, demonstrations and so forth'. To close, VOKS indicated that it was prepared to organise the entire programme from Moscow.[55]

No sooner had AERCU received this letter than it dispatched the society's general secretary, Manuel Sánchez Arcas, to a special meeting with VOKS officials in Moscow. VOKS agreed to supply Arcas with a diverse assortment of materials, including portraits of Soviet leaders, phonographic records, propaganda posters, and literature on life in the USSR. VOKS proposed that AERCU begin issuing its own propaganda journal, to be called *Cultura Soviética*, the publication of whose first issue would coincide with the jubilee. VOKS would provide AERCU with all the necessary content for the new journal. In exchange, Arcas assured VOKS that he would organise shipments of Spanish literature and other Republican cultural products for use in Soviet expositions on the Republicans and the civil war.[56]

Throughout the summer of 1937, VOKS continued to vigorously push its agenda for the early November propaganda campaign in the Republic. At times, the agency indicated disappointment that its allies at AERCU were not sufficiently zealous in their preparations for the approaching anniversary:

> A month has passed since you left Moscow and we haven't even heard if the return trip went well. As agreed during your visit in Moscow, we are beginning the shipments of various sorts of materials. What progress has been made on your end?[57]

A month later, when no reply had been received in Moscow, the VOKS functionary could barely control his frustration:

It is simply incomprehensible to us that we have heard nothing from you in over two months. We await the agreed upon shipments from Spain as well as an update on your preparations.[58]

With this letter, as with the correspondence sent earlier in the summer of 1937, VOKS diligently forwarded large amounts of materials to AERCU, including books on Soviet architecture and music, copies of the French-language daily, *Revue de Moscou*, and dozens of articles on all aspects of modern Russia.[59] The Moscow agency designed a propaganda flyer that they instructed AERCU to distribute during the jubilee. The proposed sheet mixed Soviet and Republican imagery, quotations by Stalin, and portraits of Soviet (though not Spanish Republican) leaders.[60] At the same time, VOKS made dozens of shipments of propaganda materials to the two Soviet diplomatic delegations and to the main AUS chapters in Madrid, Barcelona, and Valencia.[61]

If VOKS had feared that its recruitment of Arcas and support of AERCU would come to naught, the agency's doubts and apprehensions were soon quelled. Arcas's summer-long silence was not for want of devotion to the Soviet cause. The AERCU secretary had spent the summer collaborating with the AUS to establish an umbrella committee to oversee all Republican observations of the twentieth anniversary.[62] The result of these efforts was the founding, on 11 September 1937, of the *Comisión Nacional de Homenaje a la URSS en su XX Aniversario* (National Commission to Honour the USSR on its Twentieth Anniversary).[63] This body brought together some twenty social and political organisations whose professed purpose was the widest possible diffusion of pro-Soviet propaganda on the occasion of the twentieth anniversary of the Russian Revolution. Headed by the Madrid AUS, the commission included various political, labour, and intellectual groups that spanned the left and far-left spectrum of the Republic. Among those represented were the *Federación Anarquista Ibérica*-

Confederación Nacional del Trabajo (Iberian Anarchist Federation – National Confederation of Labour or FAI-CNT), PCE, *Partido Socialista Obrero Español* (Spanish Socialist Workers Party or PSOE), *Partido Unión Republicano* (Union Republican Party), *Partido Sindicalista* (Syndicalist Party), *Alianza de las Juventudes* (Alliance of Youth), *Izquierda Republicana* (Republican Left), *Alianza de Intelectuales Antifascistas* (Alliance of Antifascist Intellectuals), *Mujeres Libres* (Free Women), *Mujeres Antifascistas* (Anti-fascist Women, *Casa de Cultura Popular* (House of Popular Culture), and *Esquerra Valenciana* (Valencian Left).[64]

Between the activities of the commission and the increased shipments of propaganda materials from Moscow, the November commemorations in Loyalist Spain nearly rivalled those occurring in the USSR. Far from merely scheduling events on 7 November, the commission declared a 'Week of Homage to the USSR', celebrating twenty years of Soviet rule.[65] Prior to this, on 21 October, there occurred the by then familiar ceremony marking the departure for the USSR of a delegation of Spanish workers, an event given extensive coverage in the press.[66]

On 1 November, the commission unveiled an exposition of Soviet graphic arts in Valencia, while a separate installation in that city commemorated the centenary of Pushkin's death. In Madrid, a similar propaganda exposition opened, entitled 'Twenty Years of Struggle in the USSR for the Peace and Wellbeing of the People', while Soviet flags were hung in the Puerta del Sol alongside giant posters depicting Lenin and Stalin.[67] The Madrid daily *Claridad* proclaimed that 'All of Madrid's souls are united today in a single cry: ¡*Viva la Unión Soviética*!'[68]

The second day was given over to a series of conferences and lectures, including one by a member of the May Day delegation of the previous spring. In the evening, a gala concert of Soviet music was given in Valencia, broadcast by radio to the rest of the country. The third day, 3 November, was dedicated to

Soviet cinema, and included not only screenings of several recent Soviet films in Valencia theatres, but also lectures on the theory and function of the cinema in the USSR. The following day, 4 November, was organised around the theme of childhood and education. This was not limited only to conferences on Soviet policy regarding children, but was intended to involve the children of Republican Spain, who in their schools and classrooms were required to 'demonstrate their love and admiration for the Soviet Union'.[69]

Commemoration activities on 5 November were loosely organised around the twin themes of intellectuals and higher education in the USSR. A conference and ceremony at the Universidad de Valencia examined various aspects of this topic, and its proceedings were broadcast nationwide via radio. The sixth day of the Week of Homage was dedicated primarily to women – their role in Soviet society and their potential role in a postwar Spanish Republic. A series of lectures, films, and expositions on women in the USSR took place in several Republican cities, with the proceedings directed by one or more women's organisations, including *Mujeres Antifascistas* (Antifascist Women), *Mujeres Libres* (Free Women), and the *Unión de Muchachas* (Girls' Union). A secondary focus of 6 November was the Red Army, which was celebrated through gatherings, graphic art, and film, though not displays of military hardware, nor by the Red Army itself, as would become the custom at the Moscow jubilees.

The week was capped by a massive public celebration in Valencia on 7 November, in which all the members of the Commission participated, and the proceedings were broadcast via radio throughout the Republic. This marathon event, which began on the morning of 7 November and continued into the early hours of 8 November, included countless speeches by Commission signatories, resolutions of friendship with the USSR, and athletic and musical performances. Officials unveiled new street signs on what was hitherto Valencia's Calle 'Conde de Peñalver': it was now 'Avenida de la Unión Soviética'.⁷⁰

The celebrations in Valencia and Madrid were nearly equalled by events occurring elsewhere in the Republican zone. Barcelona had its own commission – the *Comité Català Pro-Homentge a la URSS XXe Aniversari de la Seva Revolució* (Pro-Homage Catalan Committee for the USSR on the Twentieth Anniversary of the Revolution), an umbrella organisation that included *Acció Catalana* (Catalan Action), *Amics de Mèxic* (Friends of Mexico), *Amics de la Unió Sovètica* (Friends of the Soviet Union), CNT, *Esquerra Republicana de Catalunya*, *Estat Catalá* (Republican Left of the State of Catalonia), FAI, *Front de la Joventut* (Youth Front), *Partit Socialista Unificat de Catalunya* (Unified Socialist Party of Catalonia or PSUC), *Partit Federal Ibéric* (Federal Iberian Party) and others.⁷¹ Throughout the week, a full range of meetings, demonstrations, conferences, concerts, and lectures took place. In addition, many smaller towns and even hamlets organised events marking the anniversary, including Blanes, Guixolls, Palafrugell, la Bisbal, Figueras, Gerona, Olot, Bañolas, Farnes de la Selva, Caldas de Montbui, and Ollería.⁷²

To complement the scheduled events for the week of 1-7 November, the Commission, the AUS, and AERCU also oversaw the publication of many pamphlets and books.⁷³ Postcards illustrating a variety of contemporary Soviet settings were printed and sold, and a series of commemorative postage stamps were issued.⁷⁴ Though prepared for the jubilee, these stamps strenuously avoided the revolution itself, focusing instead, in socialist-realist depictions, on subjects such as the Volga canal, Soviet children, or worker vacations in the USSR. The AUS journal *Rusia de Hoy* issued a special anniversary issue, in addition to the already mentioned first number of the AERCU journal, *Cultura Soviética*. The leftist press issued numerous special twentieth-anniversary pull-out sections, the glossiest and most unabashedly pro-communist was that of *Mundo Obrero* on 7 November. In addition, the AUS attempted to use the occasion to boost enrolment in Russian language classes offered in the larger cities.[75]

The Commission and AUS also collected tens of thousands of signatures in 'Golden Books' – open letters to the Soviet people, with dozens of pages of signatures attached, the text of which expressed congratulations on the anniversary, and gratitude for Soviet assistance to the Republic.[76] These were sent via VOKS to the Soviet authorities. Some of the golden books never left Spain,[77] while others evidently reached the archive (if not the desk) of the titular head of state Mikhail Ivanovich Kalinin.[78] Many other individual Republicans and Republican organisations wrote similar, separate messages to the Soviet leadership.[79] Not a few of these were published in the Soviet press.[80]

By any measure, the twentieth anniversary of the Russian Revolution marked the high-water mark of pro-Soviet propagandising in the Republican zone, and gave rise to the widest possible dissemination of favourable pronouncements concerning the USSR. None of these dealt in any way with the revolutionary year 1917, nor events at the Winter Palace, not even in Eisenstein's famous retelling from 1927. The jubilee celebrated Soviet-Spanish friendship and life in the USSR; its purpose was motivational, but the end goal was resistance, not revolution. Indeed, an internal AUS circular on the eve of the jubilee asserted that the commemorative week should focus in part on internal Soviet achievements, but principally on Moscow's capabilities and willingness to defend the peace in London and Geneva, and to 'effectively support democracies threatened by international fascism'.[81]

After the twentieth jubilee, Moscow's determination to pursue an energetic agitprop policy in the Republic showed signs of lagging. If in the spring and early summer of 1937 it was VOKS that vigorously advocated the cultural agenda to be pursued by

Republican friendship organisations, by October of that year the Soviet agency was being outdone, if not left behind, by the pro-Soviet Republicans themselves. A telling letter is one sent to VOKS from the Valencia chapter of AUS in mid-October 1937. In the missive, the group proposed to considerably augment not only the quantity of Soviet propaganda disseminated in the Republic, but also to aggressively target rural areas where the friendship societies had not yet penetrated. In effect, the Valencia AUS proposed a large-scale campaign to indoctrinate the uneducated masses:

> [We] would like to organise a series of expositions in the city of Valencia and in the province, and above all in the villages that still have no idea of the conquests achieved by your Socialist Construction. [We intend to] present conferences on technical and cultural topics, all of which will be accompanied by graphic expositions outlining the work in the farm, the factories, the life of the child and mother, the youth, and, in brief, make Russia familiar to all those who do not yet know her. But we need your help. We are requesting your assistance to publish pamphlets which will expose life in your country, so that the masses will realise what they are capable of once they set about realising [their goals]. You must understand how enormously important it is that, in these moments, the Spanish people be able to learn things about Russia – a knowledge which will facilitate the education of our masses and a confidence in their own powers.[82]

That VOKS never addressed the specific requests in this letter is indicative of a general shift in the Soviets' propaganda policy in the Republic. Much of the correspondence between VOKS and the main friendship society chapters in the Republic in the early fall of 1937 show that requests for materials from Moscow were rarely filled. On several occasions, instead of increasing shipments to a correspondent, VOKS instructed him to borrow materials from a neighbouring AUS or AERCU chapter.[83] Even Soviet political workers in Spain were lamenting in communications to Moscow officials that they had insufficient propaganda materials to carry out their agitation work among Soviet military personnel.[84]

The gradual decrease in the dissemination of Soviet propaganda is most evident if the Republic's twentieth anniversary celebrations are compared to the observations of the twenty-first, in November 1938. Whereas the twentieth anniversary was an event of vigorous and widespread involvement at many levels of Republican life, the twenty-first passed almost unnoticed in the rapidly shrinking loyalist zone. Regular contact between Spanish Republicans and VOKS had ended in the first months of the year, and the late 1937 downgrading of the Soviet diplomatic missions – which had earlier served as the key conduits between Moscow and the friendship societies – created a void, never to be filled. The AUS itself, with a few exceptions, had all but ceased to exist by mid-1938 – its active membership diminishing daily, its presses silent, and publication schedules abandoned.[85]

For November 1938, the dwindling Barcelona AUS issued a number of bulletins indicating plans for observances of the revolution, but few of these appeared to have taken place.[86] The Madrid AUS, the only other functioning friendship society at this late date, announced a conference on the Russian Revolution at the Ateneo.[87] This event included four days of lectures and presentations on Soviet society. Only *Mundo Obrero* covered the proceedings. Just before the anniversary, in October 1938, the fifth and final delegation of Spanish workers left the Republican zone to attend the Soviet celebrations in the first week of November. The group, composed of twenty men and women, remained in the USSR until the end of November.[88]

They were active in various events associated with the jubilee, and their participation followed in the Soviet press.[89] As at the commemorations in 1936 and 1937, a Soviet newsreel gave the Spanish group's presence in Red Square the requisite coverage. But in contrast to the exposure afforded earlier delegations, the group's activities in the Soviet Union not only went unexploited by propagandists in the Republic, they garnered only the briefest attention in the Loyalist press.[90]

CONCLUSION

By autumn 1938, the Kremlin had already deemed its propaganda activities within the shrinking Republican zone a poor return on further investment. The Spanish war would continue for another four months, but Moscow recognised that it had bet on the losing horse in this long struggle of attrition. The Soviet cultural offensive ended entirely, though few would have noticed; the captive Republican audience was becoming smaller by the day. Moscow would send one final shipment of arms to the Republic, in late December 1938, but it only briefly put off the inevitable defeat.[91]

For the Kremlin, to export the anniversary celebrations of October – to mark the Bolshevik Revolution in three consecutive years during the war – was not the same as exporting the revolution itself – neither as a process nor as an ideological end station. Where the Spanish Republic was concerned, the Soviets stood opposed to the revolution, supporting instead a centre-left bourgeois capitalist democracy.[92] The jubilees in the Republic were never intended to light a spark of revolution, nor to give encouragement to the social revolution that reached a high point in Barcelona in late 1936 and the first part of 1937. Indeed, Moscow's tight control of the anniversary programmes in Spain directly supported the broader Soviet policy of collective security with the western democracies, in place since 1935. Thus in

Spain, October was celebrated not as a socio-cultural process – but as an ossified monument. The jubilees exalted the Soviet state, its symbols and representations, but never the historical process of its foundation. The focus of celebrations was in part on the Soviet leadership, but also on broadly inclusive, deliberately vague categories that had little connection with the revolutionary events of 1917: Soviet women were held up as an achievement, as were Soviet children, Soviet higher education, Soviet cinema, Soviet music, and Soviet industry and agriculture. What was left out entirely were the nuts and bolts of the revolution: workers collectives, councils, strikes, the rights of labour, redistribution of wealth and property, and the nationalisation and collectivisation of industry and agriculture. Indeed, nearly every revolutionary activity promoted by the early Bolsheviks was left off the jubilee programme in Spain.

Equally paradoxical was that Moscow's military prowess – the one achievement of the Soviet Union that was most relevant to Spanish Republicans – was glossed over. Among the ceremonies, parades and demonstrations that commemorated October across the Republic, and over three years, none mimicked the most elemental aspect of the Red Square jubilees: the procession of military hardware. The Republic would receive from Moscow hundreds of I-15s and I-16 fighters – a total of 648 airplanes of all types – and some 350 tanks – predominantly the T-26 – the finest example of armour produced anywhere until 1938.[93] Yet this modern, highly effective war materiel, a fitting tribute to the Soviets achievement since 1917, was never paraded through Spanish squares.

The grand public celebrations of the Bolshevik revolution in Republican Spain may have been fleeting moments never to be repeated, but – as evidenced in unpublished archival documents, press reportage, memoirs, and newsreels – they remain singular events in the transnational cultural history of the Soviet Union.

The Soviets succeeded to a remarkable degree in dictating the jubilee programmes in Spain, and controlling their content. With the assistance of energetic collaborators in local front organisations, and the deep involvement of its embassy and consular staff, Moscow oversaw an exceptionally rich and diverse series of jubilee events. Indeed, the Soviets achieved greater influence and mastery in their agitprop campaigns connected with these jubilees than in any other area of their broad involvement in the Spanish Civil War.[94] The highpoint that was the twentieth anniversary jubilee, celebrated in uncounted cities and towns across the Spanish Republic, would remain unmatched in Soviet efforts elsewhere in Spain between 1936 and 1939, including on the battlefield. Yet a final paradox should now be evident: if the anniversaries may be understood as advertisements to heighten international awareness of the shift in Bolshevik strategies in the era of collective security, nonetheless, the plight of the Republic, and the largely magnanimous role played by Moscow in forestalling the nationalist victory, meant that the October jubilees took on an additional meaning unique to the circumstances of the Iberian peninsula. October 1917 became a rallying call and a source of inspiration; it made a difference to Spanish Republicans, and played no small role in their sustained, if ultimately doomed, resistance.

NOTES

1. James Parakilas, 'How Spain got a soul', in Jonathan Bellman (ed.), *The Exotic in Western Music*, University Press of New England: Lebanon, New Hampshire, 1997, pp168-72.
2. See *Bibliografía Española en Imágenes. Doce siglos de libros españoles*, Ed. Biblioteca Nacional: Madrid, 2009.
3. On the early history of the PCE, see Daniel Kowalsky, *La Unión Soviética y la guerra civil Española: una revisión crítica*, Critica: Barcelona, 2003, pp18-23.

4. Gerald H. Meaker, *The Revolutionary Left in Spain, 1914-1923*, Stanford University Press: Stanford, 1974, pp99-108.
5. *Ibid.*, pp128-9. May Day of 1918 saw the single-most impressive pro-Bolshevik demonstration of the period. *Ibid.*, p208.
6. Correspondence between Spain and the Vsesoiuznoe Obshchestvo Kul'turnoi Sviazi s zagranitsei (All-Union Society for Cultural Relations with Foreign Countries or VOKS) began several weeks after the tenth jubilee, on 29 November 1927. This came in the form of a query from the Guerrera travel agency in Barcelona, whose clients were interested in tourism to the USSR. Gosudarstvennyi arkhiv Rossiiskoi Federatsii (State Archive of the Russian Federation or GARF), f. 5283, op. 7, d. 666, l. 51. Useful accounts of early Spanish political tourism include V.V. Kuleshova, *Ispaniia I SSSR: Kulturnye sviazi*, Nauka: Moscow, 1975, pp49-82; Luis Lavaur, 'El viaje a la Rusia Soviética en los años treinta', *Ayeres: Cuadernos de Historia*, Vol. 4 No. 8, June 1994, pp35-45; Maria de Los Angeles Egido León, 'Del paraíso soviético al peligro marxista. La Unión Soviética en la España republicana (1931-1939)', *Cuadernos de Historia Contemporanea*, No. 10, 1988, pp139-154.
7. Kowalsky, *op. cit.*, pp13-17.
8. The now classic study on mid-1930s collective security is Jonathan Haslam, *The Soviet Union and the struggle for collective security in Europe, 1933-1939*, Macmillan: London, 1984.
9. Remarkably, the same conundrum that lay behind Stalin's reluctance to intervene in Spain would come to dominate the historiography of the war, indeed, for several generations of scholars. That Soviet policy in Spain was counter-revolutionary, and strictly advocated support of the capitalist, bourgeois Republic, did not prevent it from being condemned in much of the literature for attempting to 'sovietise' Spain – that is, to convert it into a people's democracy in the style of post-1945 Eastern Europe. On the other hand, the Troskyist reading of the war faulted the Soviets for destroying the revolution in Spain – and with it the Republic's most spirited defence. Meanwhile, the Republican mainstream and its supporters denounced the Soviets for providing insufficient aid: supplying only enough weaponry to keep the Republic alive, but not to win the war. The debate is well covered in Paul Corthorn, 'Cold War Politics in Britain and the Contested Legacy of the Spanish Civil War', *European History Quarterly*, Vol. 44 No. 4, 2014, pp678-702.

10. Arkhiv Prezidenta Rossiiskoi Federatsii (Presidential Archive of the Russian Federation or APRF), f. 3, op. 65, d. 221, l. 33.
11. Ángel Viñas, *La soledad de la República*, Crítica: Barcelona, 2006, p86.
12. APRF, f. 3, op. 65, d. 221, l. 34.
13. For a succinct presentation of Stalin's motives, see Ángel Viñas, 'September 1936: Stalin's decision to support the Spanish Republic', in Jim Jump (ed.), *Looking Back on the Spanish Civil War*, Lawrence & Wishart: London, 2010, pp146-9.
14. Viñas, *op. cit.*, pp373-98.
15. On the policy of non-intervention, see David Cattell, *Soviet Diplomacy and the Spanish Civil War*, University of California Press: Berkeley, 1957.
16. Declassified archival materials flesh out the initiation of military support: APFR, f. 3, op. 65, d. 221, l. 97-101. Decades earlier, a Soviet official publication had discussed key aspects of the dispatch of arms to Spain: *Istoriia vtoroi mirovoi voiny*, vol. II, Voennoe izdat.: Moscow, 1974, p54, p137.
17. See Kowalsky, *op. cit.*, pp133-52.
18. See Daniel Kowalsky, 'The Soviet cinematic offensive in the Spanish Civil War', *Film History*, Vol. 19 No. 1, 2007, pp7-19 and the same author's 'La ofensiva cinematográfica soviética en la guerra civil española', *Archivos de la Filmoteca*, No. 60-61, 2008, pp50-77.
19. The general topic of Soviet celebrations receives thorough analysis in Karen Petrone, *Life has become more joyous, comrades: Celebrations in the Time of Stalin*, Indiana University Press: Bloomington, 2000. On the late 1930s upswing in celebration activity, see pp14-15.
20. Kowalsky, *La Unión Soviética y la guerra civil Española*, p212.
21. Daniel Kowalsky, 'Operation X: Soviet Russia and the Spanish Civil War', *Bulletin of Spanish Studies: Hispanic Studies and Researches on Spain, Portugal and Latin America*, Vol. 91 No. 1-2, 2014, p168. On the arrival of the International Brigades, see Hugh Thomas, *The Spanish Civil War*, Simon & Schuster: New York, 1984 (3rd ed.), p456.
22. See *Mono Azul*, 29 October 1936. The journal was the principal mouthpiece of the Alianza de Intelectuales Antifascistas (Alliance of Antifascist Intellectuals). See also Carlos Fernandez Cuenca, *La Guerra de España y el Cine*, Volume I, Ed. Nacional: Madrid, 1972, pp297-324.

23. For the most complete history and analysis of VOKS, see Jean-François Fayet, *Voks. le laboratoire helvétique. Histoire de la diplomatie culturelle soviétique l'entre-deux-guerres*, Georg: Chêne-Bourg, 2014.
24. On Soviet-Spanish diplomacy during the war, see Kowalsky, *La Unión Soviética y la guerra civil Española*, pp24-72, and the same author's forthcoming pair of articles, 'Des espoirs de la diplomatie' and 'Désespoirs des diplomates', *Slavica Occitania*, special issue edited by D. Samson Normand, Vol. 44, 2018.
25. Sofiia Antonov-Ovseenko to VOKS, 31 October 1936, GARF, f. 5283, op. 7, d. 840, l. 180.
26. For a discussion of the broader euphoria that gripped the Republic in the last three months of 1936, and the role of the USSR therein, see Edward H. Carr, *The Comintern and the Spanish Civil War*, Pantheon: New York, 1984, pp32-4.
27. One of the Soviet invitations for a Spanish workers' delegation sent to the Bilbao AUS is preserved in Archivo Histórico Nacional – Sección Guerra Civil, Salamanca (National Historical Archive, Civil War Section, Salamanca or AHN-SGC), PS Bilbao, caja 253, exp. 11, doc. 29.
28. *Mundo Obrero*, 22 October 1936.
29. *Mundo Obrero* devoted a large feature to the Soviets' 'enthusiastic' reception of the Spaniards at Red Square on the anniversary date, 7 November (*Mundo Obrero*, 8 November 1936). The paper gave identical coverage to the group's activities in Leningrad several days later (*Mundo Obrero*, 12 and 14 November 1936). *Heraldo de Madrid* reported their activities in Moscow in the edition of 7 November 1936.
30. The newsreel, entitled *XIX Anniversaire de la Révolution D'Octobre 1917-1936* (The XIX Anniversary of the Russian Revolution, 1917-1936), and preserved in the Filmoteca Española, was distributed during the war by the Juventut Socialista Unificada de Catalunya (The Unified Socialist Youth of Catalonia). For a brief discussion, see Alfonso del Amo and Maria Luisa Ibañez, *Catálogo General del cine de la guerra civil*, Editorial de la Filmoteca Española: Madrid, 1996, p279.
31. AHN-SGC, PS Bilbao, caja 253, exp. 11, doc. 62.
32. The archive of the Bilbao AUS reveals that the group received many more letters declining the invitation than accepting. AHN-SGC, PS Bilbao, caja 253, exp. 11, docs. 65-85.

33. *Chapaev* received its Spanish premiere on 2 November 1936 in Madrid. The same week, Eisenstein's *The General Line* opened in Bilbao. AHN-SGC, PS Bilbao, caja 253, exp. 11, doc. 20.
34. *Mundo Obrero*, 29 October 1936.
35. *Mundo Obrero*, 31 October 1936.
36. *Heraldo de Madrid*, 7 November 1936.
37. *Claridad*, 9 April 1937.
38. *Izvestiia*, 26 April 1937.
39. *Claridad*, 3, 13, and 21 May 1937.
40. *Izvestiia*, 4, 9, and 29 May 1937.
41. *Mundo Obrero* devoted nearly the entire issue on 1 May 1937 to a spread entitled, 'Twenty Years in the Soviet Union'.
42. *Claridad*, 2 and 23 May 1938; 2 June 1938. *Mundo Obrero*, 1 and 5 May 1938; 2 June 1938.
43. One such event took place in Valencia on 14 June 1936, where the AUS arranged for members of the delegation to give speeches on their experiences. See *Claridad*, 7 June 1936, and *Mundo Obrero*, 14 June 1937.
44. *Claridad*, 10 June 1937.
45. The presenter was Pau Balsells. GARF, f. 5283, op. 7, d. 1016, l. 31.
46. *Rusia de Hoy*, 3rd epoch, 1 Aug 1937, pp14-15.
47. Barcelona AUS to VOKS, 5 June 1937. GARF, f. 5283, op. 7, d. 1016, l. 29-30
48. Sofiia Antonov-Ovseenko to VOKS, 31 October 1936. GARF, f. 5283, op. 7, del. 840, l. 180.
49. For example, the above-mentioned appearance by the Soviet economic attaché at one such event in December 1936. See Stachevsky's report from 14 December 1936, circulated among the entire Soviet leadership. Rossiiskii gosudarstvennyi voennyi arkhiv (Russian State Military Archive or RGVA), f. 33987, op. 3, d. 853, l. 322.
50. The role of women in Soviet society was a frequent topic of the Soviet cultural propaganda disseminated in Spain. In 1937, the AUS attempted to mimic the Soviet Day of Women by organizing conferences, screening films, and sending press notices to local papers. On these events, see AHN-SGC, PS Barcelona-87.
51. VOKS worked with the Barcelona consulate to disseminate cultural materials on Pushkin, for the expressed purpose of a large celebration of the poet's life in early 1937. VOKS to Consulate of the USSR, 4 January 1937. GARF, f. 5283, op. 7, d. 840, 179.

52. *Mundo Obrero*, 19 March 1937.
53. *Mundo Obrero*, 24 February 1937; *Claridad*, 24 February 1938. The celebrations in the Republic of the 1938 anniversary of the founding of the Red Army were significantly more visible than those of the year before. The 1938 date was the occasion for one of the larger displays of pro-Soviet propagandizing in the last fourteen months of the war. On 23 February 1938, the Madrid AUS staged a large gathering at the Cine Monumental, complete with the usual panoply of dignitaries and guest speakers. The record of the event is preserved at AHN-SGC, PS Madrid-2134, leg. 3042.
54. *Izvestiia*, 24 January 1937.
55. VOKS to AERCU, 25 May 1937. GARF, f. 5283, op. 7, d. 845, l. 122.
56. VOKS internal memo regarding Arcas's visits to the Moscow organization on 20 and 22 June 1937. GARF, f. 5283, op. 7, d. 1015, l. 94-96.
57. VOKS to AERCU, 16 August 1937. GARF, f. 5283, op. 7, l. 83-84.
58. VOKS to AERCU, 13 September 1937. GARF, f. 5283, op. 7, l. 63.
59. VOKS to AERCU, 16 August 1937. GARF, f. 5283, op. 7, l. 83-84.
60. GARF, f. 5283, op. 7, l. 74.
61. GARF, f. 5283, op. 7, d. 1014-1016.
62. AERCU to VOKS, 17 September 1937. GARF, f. 5283, op. 7, l. 41.
63. The founding of the commission is discussed in thorough detail in San Roman Sevillano, *Los amigos de la Unión Soviética: Propaganda política en España (1933-1938)*, PhD dissertation, Salamanca, 1993, pp155-63.
64. The original manifesto of the commission was published in the first number of AERCU's journal, *Cultura Soviética*, in November 1937. The documents chronicling the evolution of this body are assembled in the record of the commission, 'Libro de Actas de la Comisión Nacional para la celebración del XX Aniversario' ('Book of Acts of the National Commission for celebration of the XX Anniversary'). The commission was also quick to point out its unity and purpose to the Soviet authorities. On 3 October, the group sent Soviet president Mikhail Kalinin a detailed, three-page letter outlining its intentions and listing all the participating parties. Rossiiskii gosudarstvennyi arkhiv sotsial'no-politicheskoi istorii [Russian State Archive of Socio-Political History – RGASPI) (formerly Rossiiskii Tsentr Khraneniia i Izucheniia Dokumentov Noveishei Istorii, or RTsKhIDNI) f. 78, d. 667, l. 18.

65. This outline of the events between 1 and 7 November 1937 was culled from the principal unpublished archival collection on the week-long celebration; AHN-SGC, PS Barcelona-87, including newspaper articles from *El Sol*, *La Vanguardia* and *La Voz Valenciana*, all from Valencia, and *Mundo Obrero* and *Claridad* in Madrid; and San Romano Sevillano, *op. cit.*, pp163-5.
66. *Mundo Obrero*, *Claridad*, *La Vanguardia*, 22 October 1937.
67. AHN-SGC, PS Madrid-1187, leg. 3101.
68. *Claridad*, 1 November 1937.
69. The words of San Roman Sevillano, who has worked most closely with the AUS and Homage documents at AHN-SGC; *op. cit.*, p164.
70. *Ibid.*, p167. On the same date, according to this source, the Gran Via Madrileña had already become known as 'Avenida de Rusia'.
71. Documentation on the Barcelona Homage Committee is preserved at AHN-SGC, PS Madrid-630, leg. 875, and PS Barcelona-770.
72. On the twentieth anniversary events in these and other remote presidios, see San Roman Sevillano, *op. cit.*, 167-9, and the same author's 'Valencia, 1937: Fallas para el XX aniversario de la URSS', *Historia y Vida*, No. 348, 1997, pp112-23. Also, AHN-SGC, PS Barcelona-770.
73. These included, for example, the short pamphlet '20 Años de Solidaridad humana en la URSS'.
74. Examples of the commemorative postcards and stamps are preserved in AHN-SGC, Tarjetas y Sellos.
75. AHN-SGC, PS Madrid-1187, leg. 3101.
76. Signatures for the golden books began to be solicited in August 1937, and continued up to the end of October. The AUS announced the signature drive in the August issue of *Rusia de Hoy*, No. 2.
77. Some of the golden books circulated at the front were likely captured before they could be sent. They are preserved at AHN-SGC, PS Madrid-83, leg. 1050, exp. 26-30; PS Madrid-410, leg. 3259, exp. 32; PS Barcelona-798.
78. Kalinin's archive at RGASPI contains several bulky folders of these personal letters. RGASPI, f. 78, d. 667, ll. 27-33.
79. RGASPI, f. 78, d. 667, ll. 39-220.
80. *Izvestiia* published open letters from the Republic on 1, 4, 5, 7, and 10 November 1937.
81. Amigos de la Unión Soviética, 'Informe al Comité Provincial de Madrid', October 1937. AHN-SGC, PS Madrid, caja 445.

82. Valencia AUS to VOKS, 20 October 1937. GARF, f. 5283, op. 7, d. 1016, l. 10.
83. VOKS to Barcelona AUS, 17 August 1937. GARF, f. 5283, op. 7, d. 1016, l. 28.; VOKS to Barcelona AUS, 22 October 1937. GARF, f. 5283, op. 7, d. 1016, ll. 23-24.
84. Report to Voroshilov, 22 October 1937. RGVA, f. 33987, op. 3, d. 1033, ll. 174-183. Reproduced in Mary Habeck and Ronald Radosh, *Spain Betrayed: The Soviet Union in the Spanish Civil War*, Yale University Press: New Haven, 2001, p483.
85. On the gradual decline and collapse of the Spanish AUS, see San Roman Sevillano, *op. cit.*, pp179-80.
86. AHN-SGC, PS Barcelona, caja 102, exp. 1, Boletines 11-14.
87. AHN-SGC, PS Madrid, caja 445, leg. 3594, doc. 106.
88. *Pravda*, 1 December 1938. San Roman Sevillano, in his otherwise excellent dissertation, mistakenly claims that the fifth delegation never left Spain, p180.
89. As was the case with all foreign delegations to the USSR, their activities were closely supervised and monitored by the authorities. A detailed file covering all aspects of their trips may be read in RGASPI, f. 78, d. 689, ll. 4-130.
90. The lone article on their trip appeared in *Mundo Obrero* on 12 November 1938. There were apparently no earlier reports of their arrival, reception or itinerary in the USSR.
91. The late dispatch of some $55 million worth of Soviet arms, transferred on seven ships, was for many years considered a myth, yet today declassified documents from the Military Archive confirm that this did indeed take place. The logistics of the operation, and contents of the delivery, down to the precise number of shells (1,382,540), are revealed in manifests in RGVA, f. 33987, op. 3, d. 1259, ll. 85-105.
92. The conclusion of nearly all commentators, and the principal subject of Burnett Bolloten, *The Spanish Civil War: Revolution and Counterrevolution in Spain, 1936-1939*, University of North Carolina Press: Chapel Hill, 1991.
93. Iurii E. Ribalkin, *Operatsiia 'X':Sovietskaia voennaia pomoshch' respublikanskoi Ispanii (1936-1939)*, 'AIRO-XX': Moscow, 2000, p44.
94. The historiography of the war in recent years has seen one scholar after another cast doubt on the Cold War-era thesis that Stalin exercised hegemony in Spain. The works of this author, summarised in 2014, have been complemented by those of Angel Viñas, Iurri

Ribalkin and, most recently, Josep Puigsech Farras, *Falsa leyenda del Kremlin. El consulado y la URSS en la Guerra Civil Española*, Biblioteca Nueva: Madrid, 2014. Farras argues that Soviet military aid to the Republic had surprisingly few strings attached, and that the Kremlin's consulate in Barcelona peddled little influence during the war.

Commemorating the October Revolution in Greece, 1918-1949

Anastasia Koukouna

From the earliest years following the October Revolution, the marking of its anniversary became a memorial day for revolutionaries all over the world. However, the study of its commemoration reveals how the meanings of October were often modified according to the shifts of the international communist movement as well as the different national and historical contexts. The commemorations of the October Revolution in Greece, where an important popular movement developed from the mid-1930s, are indicative of this trend.

From the foundation in 1918 of the Socialist Labour Party of Greece (*Sosialistiko Ergatiko Komma Ellados*, SEKE), communists in Greece regarded the anniversary of October as the most important day of international working-class memory, along with 1 May. The anniversary was marked by various public events in Athens and other Greek cities with the exception of the years when Greece was under dictatorship (1925-6 and 1936-40) or under foreign occupation (1941-4). In the first part of this chapter, I will suggest that the content and form of the celebrations followed, in a fashion, the ideological transformations of the communist party in the inter-war period. I will also show how both the ideological controversy within the party, which was particularly strong in the 1920s, and the controversy between the communists and the Trotskyists found expression in the commemorations of October. In the second part, I will discuss how the celebrations held in Athens in 1944-6 were adapted to the communists' policy of national unity. In the final section of the paper, I will study the commemorations of the anniversary that took place in the Greek countryside in 1947-8, during the Civil War.

THE COMMEMORATIONS OF OCTOBER DURING THE INTER-WAR PERIOD

During the nineteenth century and the first two decades of the twentieth, the socialist movement in Greece was particularly weak, organisationally as well as ideologically. Early Greek socialism, elaborated by a small number of intellectuals, was a mixture of utopian socialism, anarchism, jacobinism, and Christian ideals. The impact of Marx's works, and subsequently of Lenin's further elaborations, was almost insignificant during this period. Jean Longuet, in his *Encyclopédie socialiste syndicale et coopérative de l'Internationale ouvrière*, underlined the backwardness of the Greek socialist movement, comparing it to socialist movements in Serbia, Bulgaria, and Romania. According to Longuet, the weakness of Greek socialism could be explained by the predominance of pre-capitalist economic conditions in the country.[1]

The foundation of the SEKE, the first unified socialist party in the country, took place particularly late on, in November 1918, under the influence of the October Revolution and almost coinciding with its first anniversary. The SEKE, originally representing no more than a thousand organised socialists and connected to the Second International, was characterised by a strong ideological heterogeneity. At its first congress, representatives of diverse political trends, from social democracy to communism, debated at length to define the official line of the new party, which would prove to be far more reformist than revolutionary.[2] The SEKE's 'programme of current claims', voted by the first congress, included a series of demands aiming at the democratisation of political and social life and the improvement of the situation of the working class.[3]

The first left turn of the SEKE was carried out between 1919 and 1920, at a time when Soviet power was being stabilised in Russia and the communists were cutting themselves off from socialist parties in order to join the Comintern. In the aftermath of the defeated revolutions in Germany and Hungary, but also in the context of Greece's participation in the campaign of the Entente forces in Russia, the second congress of the SEKE, in April 1920, marked the beginning of the bolshevisation process in the party. This was signalled by the SEKE's association with the Communist International and by the addition, within brackets, of the adjective 'Communist' to the party's title.

October 1920 was the first time the SEKE(K) together with the General Confederation of Greek Workers (GCGW, or *Gheniki Sinomospondia Ergaton Ellados*, GSEE), commemorated the October Revolution with a public event, held at the Olympia theatre in central Athens.[4] It was a solidarity and protest gathering against Greece's participation in the allied intervention in Russia. This commemoration coincided with an election campaign in Greece and took place in a festive atmosphere.[5] Communist press reports allow us to imagine a few hundred communists, mostly workers, intellectuals, and students, and probably exclusively men, flocking with their red banners to the centre of Athens. The party's declaration on the anniversary is indicative of its left turn:

> The Greek proletariat, celebrating today the third anniversary of the Russian Revolution, promises that it will fight for the final triumph of the work of Russian workers and peasants, that it will fight to mobilise poor masses of Greece in an active

struggle in favour of Russian Soviets, in a struggle that will prepare and develop the capacity of the Greek working people to create the soviets of workers and peasants in Greece too.[6]

A year later, the party's bolshevisation was temporarily halted. This was because of the predominance within it of the social-democratic line advocating a 'long legal existence' and organisational strengthening of the party and arguing that the objective conditions for a socialist revolution in Greece were not yet sufficiently mature. This turn was crystallised during the first national conference of the SEKE(K) in February 1922. Indicative of this shift to legality and caution was the transfer of the event dedicated to the commemoration of October from a large public theatre in 1920 to the offices of the party in 1921.[7] Nevertheless, according to the leadership of the party, the October Revolution was still 'a great lesson of political education'.[8]

During this same period, either side of the defeat of the Greek army by Kemal Ataturk's troops in August 1922, the political situation in Greece was very unstable, and censorship and state repression were growing. The Central Committee of the SEKE(K) and the leaders of the GCGW had been arrested for anti-war propaganda in February 1922, while communist soldiers were imprisoned in Smyrna, accused of high treason. Thus, for the years 1922 and 1923, there were no public gatherings in Athens in honour of the anniversary, probably because of the political repression exercised by the government that had been formed after the military coup following the disaster for Greek forces in Asia Minor.

The bolshevisation of the party was completed in 1924: in February, by the exclusion of the social-democratic leaders at the SEKE's National Council, and at the end of the year by the party's third, extraordinary congress held in the presence of the Cominternian Dmitri Manuilsky. This congress decided to accept the Comintern's twenty-one conditions of admission and, the renaming of the party as the Communist Party of Greece (KKE) – Greek section of the Communist International. It also adopted the tactics of the united front and an organisational restructuring based on the principles of the Leninist party of a new type.

This new turn may be detected in the celebration of the seventh anniversary of the October Revolution, in November 1924, which was for the first time prestigious and well organised. The celebration was prepared several days earlier, with instructions given to the party members and to the members of the Young Communist League of Greece (OKNE), founded in 1922, through the columns of *Rizospastis*, the official newspaper of the party.[9] The guidelines refer mainly to the propaganda which should be developed on the occasion of the anniversary:

> This year the holiday of 7 November coincides with the so-called democratic-pacifist period that strengthens democratic prejudices and whims. That is why the comparison between bourgeois democracy and Soviets, in front of the masses of workers and peasants, as well as the comparison between the consequences that each one of these systems can have upon them, would be the best way to celebrate the overthrow of the bourgeois-democratic regime in Russia in October 1917.[10]

We can clearly discern the revolutionary shift of the party, now struggling 'for the final liberation from exploitation and oppression against Greek capitalism', against bourgeois democracy and in favour of a Soviet Greece. On 7 November 1924 *Rizospastis* was completely given over to the occasion, while the theoretical review of the party *Kommounistiki Epitheorisi* (*The Communist Review*) published translations of articles of Lenin, Victor Serge, and Alexei Rykov on the anniversary of the revolution and the achievements of the young Soviet Union.[11] *Rizospastis* also informs us that the celebration of the seventh anniversary included a visit of trade union workers, students and refugees from Asia Minor to the Soviet embassy in Athens.[12]

On the occasion of the seventh anniversary, the Greek Minister of Foreign Affairs, Georgios Roussos, visited the Soviet embassy too. This was in order to congratulate the Soviet ambassador, who had arrived in Greece in August 1924, on behalf of the government of the newly born Second Hellenic Republic.[13] In March 1924, the Greek monarchy was abolished and in the same period Greece became the first Balkan state to recognise the Soviet Union. By establishing diplomatic relations with the Soviet Union, the Greek government aimed, on the one hand, to ensure protection for Greeks living in Russia, and, on the other, to help Greek shipowners whose ships were transporting Soviet products.

The following year, from June 1925 to July 1926, the communist party was made illegal by the Pangalos dictatorship and became clandestine. At the same time, an intense inner-party crisis erupted, partly under the influence of the left opposition in the Soviet Union. In practice, the political conditions created by Greece's successive repressive regimes of the inter-war period favoured a lack of party discipline within the KKE, and discouraged internal democracy within the party. The Leninist principles of the party of a new type were adopted in 1924, but were barely applied, while factionalism was the main characteristic of the KKE's internal life, at least until the intervention of the Comintern in 1931.

In November 1926, a few months after the reversal of Pangalos' military dictatorship, the anniversary of the October Revolution coincided with the day of the general elections in Greece.[14] In these circumstances, the KKE regarded the anniversary as an opportunity to manifest its anti-bourgeois and ultra-revolutionary views:

> On this day of the ninth anniversary of the October Revolution, the bourgeoisie of our country plays the game of the expression of people's will by the elections. There is no Parliament that can save the bourgeoisie. It is rotten and in a state of dissolution. We are participating in the elections today, we are facing the electoral battle; the ballot is our weapon and the hammer-sickle is our symbol. We are convinced that the day is not far away when we will freely celebrate our own October.[15]

On the tenth anniversary in 1927, the KKE, weakened ideologically and organisationally by the inner-party crisis, did not organise any central gathering in Athens. Only some small events took place in cafés and restaurants.[16] The following year, in a period of important working-class actions and intense state repression, on the occasion of the anniversary a central gathering did take place in the hall of the trade unions, where a honorary presidium was elected comprising Stalin, Bukharin, Krupskaya, the German Thälmann, the Bulgarian Kolarov, and 'other comrades'. The KKE had just accepted the 'three period' views of the Comintern, marking a sharp turn to the left.[17]

In this same period, Greek Trotskyism grew stronger, mainly because of the constant crises afflicting the KKE. In Greece, there were two antagonistic Trotskyist organisations: the Communist Organisation of Bolshevik-Leninists of Greece – Archeio-Marxists (KOMLEA), which from 1930 was connected to the left opposition; and the Spartakos group founded by the Marxist intellectual Pantelis Pouliopoulos, a former KKE leader. In 1934, Spartakos would be renamed the Organisation of Internationalist Communists of Greece (OKDE).

Just like the KKE, Greek Trotskyists sought to appear as the real owners of the heritage of the Russian Revolution.[18] In 1931, during significant working-class mobilisations, and in an atmosphere of government prohibitions and repression, we can trace, through the papers of the Trotskyists and communists, how they disputed the organisation of the October celebrations in the assemblies of the trade unions, and finally ended up by organising separate events in Athens.[19] In the following years, communists denied any connection between the heritage of October and the Trotskyist movement. The title of an article published in the KKE's theoretical review sums up this attitude: 'The Character of the October Revolution and its counter-revolutionary evaluation by Social-Fascists and Trotskyists'.[20]

Meanwhile, in early November 1931, the Comintern put an end to the large-scale crisis within the party, known as 'faction struggle without principles', by imposing the leadership of the young Moscow-educated Nikos Zachariadis, who would remain the party's leader until the period of destalinisation. The date of Zachariadis' assumption of the leadership, which almost coincided with the October Revolution, became another important memorial day for the party. Indeed, it was sometimes presented, particularly from 1941 when Zachariadis was deported to the Dachau concentration camp, as if it were of equal importance to the October anniversary, if not indeed more important still. For example, in November 1946, *Kommounistiki Epitheorisi* contained three articles about Zachariadis, who had been released from Dachau and returned in Greece in May 1945, and only one about the anniversary of the October Revolution. The articles were 'The Personality of the Comrade N. Zachariadis in the KKE' by Yorgis Siantos; 'Zachariadis, a Champion of National Unity' by Dimitris Partsalidis; and 'Some biographical elements of N. Zachariadis' by Kostas Karayorgis. All three were written by future enemies of his within the party.

During the first half of the 1930s, the KKE grew stronger because of the ending of the inner-party crisis and the enforcement of its monolithic character. From around 1500 members in 1930, the KKE had 4000 members in 1933 and 17,500 in 1936.[21] In the national elections of June 1935, in which the KKE participated as the *Pallaïko Metopo* (All People Front), it obtained 9.6 per cent of the vote. Having just previously adopted an anti-fascist stance based on the new positions of the Comintern, on the seventeenth anniversary of October the revived KKE organised a rally in central Athens and several smaller events in deprived neighbourhoods of the Greek capital.[22] The slogans that predominated were those of the struggle against fascism and the defence of the 'Soviet Fatherland'.[23] The anti-fascist turn of the KKE would be ratified by its sixth congress in December 1935.

On 4 August 1936, the rise of the Communist Party of Greece and that of the Greek labour movement was violently disrupted by the Metaxas dictatorship, which furiously persecuted the KKE. Henceforth, most Greek communists commemorated the anniversaries of October in prison or in islands of exile, with wall newspapers, secret newspapers, and tracts, written by hand and distributed among political detainees. At the same time, the Soviet embassy in Athens continued to organise receptions and other festivities to which the leaders of the dictatorship were also invited. In November 1939, less than three months after the signing of the German-Soviet non-aggression pact, and in the new context of the Second World War, the dictator Metaxas and his wife honoured the anniversary by accepting the invitation to a reception organised by the embassy.[24] Worried about Italian provocations, the virulent anti-communist Metaxas would have calculated that good relations with the Soviet Union would probably assist Greece in maintaining its neutrality.

THE OCTOBER REVOLUTION AND THE POLICY OF NATIONAL UNITY

On 28 October 1940, the CPSU central committee sent a directive to the Comintern secretary Georgi Dimitrov, stating that the Comintern executive committee should not have published a manifesto on the occasion of the October anniversary 'because of the international situation'. According to this directive, Dimitrov had sent a telegram to all communist parties asking them to publish a commemorative communiqué attaching special importance to the peace politics of the Soviet Union.[25] However, the twenty-third anniversary could not have been publicly celebrated in Greece, as the country had just entered the Second World War against Fascist Italy.

The following year, in a telegram sent to the Communist Party of Great Britain, Dimitrov wrote that the 'heroic struggle' of the Red Army against Hitler's Germany should be placed at the heart of the campaign on the occasion of the anniversary.[26] The defence of the Soviet Union was now 'the highest duty of every worker and friend of freedom!'[27] For communists all over the world, the Soviet Union was now the 'Anti-fascist Fatherland', and this should have made a particular impression on the Greek communists who, during the Axis occupation, managed to organise and guide one of the most important resistance movements in Europe:

> The Greek people are proud, because together with the Soviet peoples, together with the peoples of Yugoslavia, theirs were the greatest sacrifices, the most heroic achievements, in the universal struggle for national freedom, for the power of the people. The Greek people are proud, because they fight next to the great allies England, America, Soviet Union for the great democratic ideals proclaimed in the Atlantic Charter.

The anniversary of the October Revolution, and its invincible Herculean strength manifested in the victories of the Red Army, are a great guarantee for the triumph of our cause. For the defeat of fascism. For the realisation of our national renewal, for the triumph of our democratic will.[28]

During the occupation, the KKE, as leader of the resistance movement, espoused patriotism and national unity rather than the struggle for working-class liberation. The National Liberation Front, founded in September 1941 at the communists' initiative, favoured the anniversary of the Greek War of Independence over that of the October Revolution. The struggle for Greek liberation was often presented as 'the new 1821' and anti-Axis mobilisations were organised on 25 March, on the occasion of the anniversary of the beginning of the Greek War of Independence.

In 1944, the twenty-seventh anniversary of October fell about a month after the liberation of Athens and a month before the battle of Athens, when the resistance movement came into collision with British troops and the Greek bourgeois political forces. During the occupation, the resistance movement had won over a majority in Greek society, but the national unity line of its leadership had drawn the movement into the trap of the Greek right and British foreign policy. While the National Liberation Front participated in the national unity government of Georgios Papandreou, in early November there arose the thorny issue of the partisans' disarmament and the creation of a national army. This was the issue that would lie behind the conflict in December. The clouds of civil war had started to overshadow the excitement of the liberation, and one could now see very clearly the impasse of the communist leadership's policy.

On the occasion of that year's October Revolution anniversary, Greek communists expressed their gratitude to the Soviet Union:

The Greek people ... feel a particular joy for the great anniversary of the peoples of the USSR, because they do not forget that their own stubborn and bloody struggle to oust the foreign occupier from their country was significantly assisted by the heavy blows of the Red Army against the Hitlerian beast in the Balkans, in Romania and in Bulgaria.[29]

However, in this new context the anniversary of October was not to be commemorated with a mass rally in central Athens, such as would follow two weeks later on the occasion of the anniversary of the party's foundation on 19 November. The force of this massive and glorious commemoration impressed the liberal intellectual George Theotokas, who wrote in his diary:

Today the KKE is celebrating the 26th anniversary of its foundation. A big rally of the party was held in the Constitution Square, with flags and emblems as in previous times. There was a quantity of red flags; Greek flags were significantly fewer, the allied flags were too little in number. The innovation was the dress code of the demonstrators. These wore a lot of red: ties, shirts, skirts, dresses. Some of them wore red woolly hats with long white tassels. This red was deep, flaming, purposely chosen to impose itself on the eye.[30]

Reinforced by the delegitimation of other political parties because of their stance during the Metaxas dictatorship and Axis occupation, as well as by the party's own line of anti-fascist unity, the KKE had won over broad sections of the population and had more than 400,000 members in 1944.[31] On the occasion of the October anniversary, this massive communist party organised, instead of a mass rally, various local and sectoral events in different quarters of the capital, in an atmosphere of enthusiasm and sympathy for the great ally.[32] The KKE leadership would have rejected the idea of a mass rally to mark the occasion so as not to provoke Greek reactionary forces. Greek communists had to make it clear that the Great October Revolution was not at this point a model to be followed, and wanted to place the emphasis on the USSR's role in the Second World War, definitely not on the proletarian character of October. Celebrations of the 1944 anniversary took place in smaller Greek cities too. In Lamia, for example, where the KKE and the National Liberation Front had conquered great influence, the Soviet officer of the Allied Mission gave a speech in front of thousands of people.[33]

In Athens, on the occasion of the same anniversary, a huge poster with Stalin's image and the inscription 'Freedom to the people' was posted at the central Syntagma Square, while smaller portraits of Stalin were posted throughout the city. These portraits were destroyed on the night of 8 November by members of nationalist anti-communist organisations, who were already at war with the Resistance, even prior to the country's liberation.[34] Within less than a month, the members of these organisations, together with British troops, would fight the Resistance partisans in the Battle of Athens – an episode anticipating the forthcoming Cold War.

Within a year, from November 1944 to November 1945, the political situation in Greece had shifted radically. This time it had shifted against the KKE and the National Liberation movement. The military defeat of the left, in December 1944, and the signing of the Varkiza agreement in February 1945 had signalled the beginning of the reorganisation of the bourgeois state. Even more than this, what historians refer to as the white terror had spread, mainly in the countryside.[35] Violence and various forms of persecution and repression were now the everyday lot of the left's supporters.

In this specific context, in November 1945, the October anniversary was organised not by the KKE, but by the Greek-Soviet

League.[36] Founded a few months earlier, in July 1945, this organisation assembled not only communists but also liberals and social democrats, who were attracted to the prestige acquired by the Soviet Union during the war. In this commemorative event, with a rich artistic programme featuring both Greek and Soviet content, the speakers were not communist party members, but intellectuals and supporters of democracy, who had collaborated with the National Liberation Front during the occupation. The KKE's clear intention was not to organise a celebration for a narrow partisan audience, but to give the event the character of a broader front. Similar events were scheduled by the Greek-Soviet League in Piraeus and other Greek cities.

The rich artistic content of 1945 celebrations demonstrates that the KKE was now a genuine mass party which had managed to influence a large number of intellectuals, and exercise a wider cultural programme for the masses. The celebrations organised by the Greek-Soviet League included plays, dance performances, recitations of poems, exhibitions, and small concerts. Moreover, in November 1945, the film *Lenin in October*, by the SOV-FILM company, was screened with great success at the 'Ideal' cinema in the centre of the Greek capital.[37] The Theatre Company of United Artists, connected to the KKE and to the National Liberation Front, played a significant role in the organisation of such events.[38]

The celebration of the anniversary that year had a much more patriotic content. The Soviet Union was no longer a model for the overthrow of capitalism, but the great ally which helped other nations to obtain liberty and independence. The president of the Greek-Soviet League, Professor Nikos Kitsikis, underlined this aspect in his speech:

> The unfeigned love of the Greek people for the peoples of the Soviet Union, that makes today's huge gathering vibrate with excitement, is a response to the feelings of friendship that

Russia always showed to Greece. ... Together with our friendship, so often tested, for our other major allies, Great Britain, the United States and France, we consider the love of our people for the peoples of the Soviet Union as a major national asset that will offer precious help for the reconstruction of our country and for the elaboration of a right and honest foreign policy that will ensure not only our national interests, but also the peace in the Balkans that is so necessary for the happiness of all Balkan peoples.[39]

By using the phrase 'the feelings of friendship that Russia always showed to Greece', the president of the Greek-Soviet League referred to the supposed aid that the Russian Empire offered to Greeks during their independence wars in the nineteenth century. Similar arguments were used by Michalis Kyrkos, a non-communist politician of the Political Coalition of the Parties of the National Liberation Front on the occasion of the same anniversary in 1946:

Besides, not only the ties of the latest common struggle connect the Greek to the Soviet people. These ties are older. They start at the time of the Greek Empire of Byzantium and they continue, through the Turkish conquest, until our sacred struggle for Independence, in which the contribution of the Russian people was powerful and precious.[40]

Another argument that could reinforce the pro-Russian sentiments of Greek society during the early post-war period, but which was never explicitly stated by supporters of the left, was the sense of belonging to the same religion, to the common Orthodox faith.

In November 1946, on the twenty-ninth anniversary of October, the Greek civil war was already a reality in the countryside. In February of that year, the Second Plenum of the KKE central committee had deliberated whether to resort to limited violence as a defence against the violence that had been exercised against the left's supporters since the signing of the Varkiza agreement. Six weeks later, communists and their allies abstained from the general elections of March 1946. On the eve of the elections, an attack by a group of partisans on the gendarmerie station of Litohoro in northern Greece took place. Since June, the Greek parliament had passed the so-called Third Resolution 'on emergency measures against those threatening public order and integrity of the state', while partisan units were coming together in mountainous areas. This period is characterised, on the one hand, by the general tolerance of the KKE and its front organisations, and on the other hand by the furious repression of its members and supporters. However, despite the extent of the conflict, reconciliation was still the official political line of the communist party. By following a 'war and peace strategy', the KKE wanted only to protect the lives of its followers and to reach an honest compromise, which would have given it the opportunity to participate in the political life of the country.[41]

In this context of conflict, Greek communists now saw in the Soviet Union the 'secure bastion for people's peace, security, freedom and independence' – this according to the declaration of the Soviet party published on the front page of *Rizospastis*.[42] The USSR was also a model for development and dignity:

> We are welcoming with real joy the twenty-ninth anniversary of the October Revolution, its achievements, its triumphs. As the democratic nation that we are, as a people who fought for independence, as a people at this moment under foreign control, we see in these triumphs the triumphs of all peoples, of all mankind. We feel most strongly their impact and their present importance as we can see crystallised the huge projects

of peaceful reconstruction, the projects of the new five-year plan, while here our life is paralysed under a regime of terror, of civil war and of economic exploitation – of Greek and foreign origin.[43]

The celebrations for the 1946 anniversary were again organised by the Greek-Soviet League and lasted an entire week. They mainly featured small art events and lectures, given by intellectuals who were not communist party members but 'fellow travellers'. In these events, according to *Rizospastis*, a few hundred people gathered, among them cadres of the Soviet embassy in Athens. But entry was 'only by personal invitation', apparently for reasons of security.[44]

A reception at the Soviet embassy in Athens was also organised. Here, high-ranking communist cadres – perhaps for the first and definitely for the last time – met with prime minister Konstantinos Tsaldaris, an emblematic figure of the conservative party, and with other politicians of the bourgeois parties, as well as with senior members of the Greek army and security forces and the British and American ambassadors.[45] A few months earlier, during the Paris peace conference, the USSR had consented to the ceding to Greece of the Dodecanese islands, which had been occupied by the Italians since 1912.

On the same anniversary, while communist partisans in the countryside were facing firing squads, and thousands were imprisoned or incarcerated in camps, the Trotskyists of the Communist Internationalist Party of Greece (4th International), who had distanced themselves from the KKE's struggle against Greek bourgeois forces and the Americans, considered the commemoration of October to be an opportunity to attack the communists: 'The road to Socialism had been blocked until now by the historic betrayal of international Social Democracy and international Stalinism, guided by the logic of their particular interests which are alien and hostile to the interests of the World Revolution'.⁴⁶

COMMEMORATING OCTOBER IN FREE GREECE

By November 1947, the armed conflict had spread all over the Greek countryside. In June of the same year, KKE central committee member Miltiadis Porphyrogenis, had, from the rostrum of the eleventh congress of the French Communist Party in Strasbourg, announced the goal to create 'a free and Democratic Greece with its own government and its own institutions' in areas under the control of the Democratic Army of Greece. In August, the constitutional acts of 'Free Greece' – the name given the territory liberated by the partisans – were published. Free Greece extended over the mountainous regions of Epirus, central and western Macedonia, and Peloponnese. Its borders changed frequently according to the evolution of military operations, but the liberation of a large city was never to be achieved. The populations residing in the regions of Free Greece were mainly peasants, particularly weakened by the experience of occupation and the 'white terror'.

In Free Greece, and in the sections of the Democratic Army of Greece, from the spring of 1947, when the civil war was widespread, to the communists' military defeat in the summer of 1949, various anniversaries were commemorated, and celebrations and festivities organised, whenever the military situation allowed. These events had several aims, such as the political, ideological, and historical education of both the partisans and the people, as well as aiming to raise the morale of the former and instill confidence in the latter. The partisans' leadership had established a Bureau of Enlightenment of the general headquarters of the Democratic Army of Greece for purposes of political education and propaganda. The bureau saw in the celebration of the anniversaries an instrument of political conviction and education, and as well as cultural events and articles in the Democratic Army press, there were even specific publications published by 'Free Greece', the partisans' official publishing house.[47]

Among the occasions celebrated were International Women's Day and 1 May, as well as anniversaries relating to the struggle of the Democratic Army, for example those of the establishment of the provisional democratic government and the Democratic Army's unification, or the foundation of the National Liberal Front. The anniversary of the KKE's foundation was particularly celebrated in November 1947 and November 1948, because the party was now the only political and organisational leadership of the partisans. In some villages, partisans even celebrated the date of 6 December, the traditional feast of St Nicholas, who had the name of the Greek communist leader Nikos Zachariadis.[48]

With the organisation of artistic events and popular banquets, special emphasis was accorded the dates of 28 October, the day of Greece's entry into the Second World War and of the foundation of the Democratic Army, and 15 March, the anniversary of the Greek war of independence. In this way, the KKE leadership insisted on the national liberation character of the struggle of the Democratic Army, for the independence of Greece against US imperialism and the 'local fascist clan'.[49]

This may explain why, during the war, the anniversary of the October Revolution seemed to be of secondary importance. It was certainly commemorated in the press of the Provisional Democratic Government and Democratic Army, but there are very few traces of popular celebrations. The anniversary articles that did appear in the communist and Democratic Army press in most cases underlined the role of the Soviet Union in the new context of the Cold War:

> The 30th anniversary of the Soviet Revolution finds the world divided again into two camps. ... In the face of this situation,

the rallying and organising of democratic and anti-imperialist forces in each country and the co-ordination of their action at an international level are necessary. The people of Greece find themselves in one of the most advanced outposts of the anti-imperialist and democratic forces and there they do their duty. ... Tortured and fighting humanity turns its head with hope towards Moscow.[50]

The international role of the Soviet Union was furthermore propagated via the publication in a brochure of Molotov's speech on the occasion of the thirtieth anniversary of October.[51] In any case, Greek partisans fighting against US imperialism looked on the USSR as 'a sure guarantee that all the efforts of the imperialists to enslave the peoples and to establish their world domination will miserably fail'.[52]

A large celebration on the thirtieth anniversary in 1947 took place at the Military School of Officers of the general headquarters of the Democratic Army. This turned into a 'national celebration event' with traditional songs and dances; in the Democratic Army ideological-political work and entertainment were very often connected.[53] Dancing, music, and theatre were the commonest and simplest means of entertainment aimed at raising the morale of a popular army whose soldiers were 'often without bread, without good clothing'.[54] In a situation of continuing armed conflict, entertainment was also a means of distracting partisans 'from their terrible memories and from their horrible thoughts'.[55]

The following year, the KKE leadership celebrated the thirty-first anniversary of October with an official event at the general headquarters of the Democratic Army. At this event, the lieutenant general of the Democratic Army, Kostas Karayorgis, compared the partisans to the Bolsheviks and praised them for their courage.[56] The partisan leadership also commemorated the foundation of the Red Army, which was supposed to be a model for the Democratic Army. Nevertheless, among the partisans' units and in the liberated areas, it seems that commemorations of October – when they took place at all – were limited to small-scale lectures without any festive aspect. For example, in November 1948 the students of the People's School of Teacher Education of the Peloponnese were given a lecture on the revolution's meaning, after having attended mass.[57]

In any case, during the civil war, the anniversaries were imbued with a national liberation and anti-imperialist character. This matched that which the KKE leadership sought to attach to the cause defended by the Democratic Army. As a pamphlet of the communist organisation of Kilkis put it, 'the Greek people, by celebrating today the thirtieth anniversary of the Great October Revolution, will further strengthen its resistance against the American and British conquerors who violate our freedom and our national independence'.[58] Any parallels between the struggle of the Democratic Army and the October Revolution were drawn mainly to raise the partisans' morale.

After its military defeat in August 1949, the KKE and its 60,000 members and sympathisers who sought refuge in the Soviet Union and people's democracies, continued to celebrate the anniversary of October, but in a completely different social and political environment. Defeated and in exile, they would henceforth look on this more as the national anniversary of the country which had helped them escape the vengeance of their enemies, than as a vision of the revolution soon to become reality. Moreover, the anniversary was also an opportunity to demonstrate their gratitude to their newly adopted countries by participating in their reconstruction:

> As guests, as co-builders of Socialism in this country, we have to take an active part in this campaign for the Great

October. We have to participate in the great productive effort of this People's Republic that has embraced us. ... Our factory workers must raise high the levels of production. Our collective farmers must make greater efforts for gathering the autumn crop. Our students in schools must achieve a better performance. Workers must work more hours in honour of the Great October.[59]

From its foundation in 1918, the KKE had regarded the anniversary of October as one of the most important memorial days of the communist calendar. However, the form and content of the commemorations were often modified according to political shifts, which in most cases followed the changes in the strategy of the international communist movement. Thus, if in 1920 the anniversary had been the occasion to promote the slogan of a Soviet Greece, in 1945-6 it was far more the opportunity to honour the USSR's victory over fascism than to recall the Bolsheviks' revolutionary overthrow of capitalism, which was not now a model to imitate. Especially during the Resistance (1941-44) and the Civil War (1947-49), communists in Greece had seemed to favour national and not communist memorial days, in order to demonstrate their policy of national unity and underline the national liberation character of their struggle against the Axis powers and then the British and Americans. During these periods, even specifically communist commemorations, like the anniversary of October, seemed to have relinquished their socialist content and acquired a new patriotic one. The specificities of the KKE included a period of underground struggle which lasted almost four decades, and further research into the party's politics of historical memory could contribute significantly to our understanding of national and international communist tactics and strategy, and of the relations between the central leadership of the international communist movement and its periphery.

NOTES

1. Jean Longuet, *Encyclopédie socialiste syndicale et coopérative de l'Internationale ouvrière*, vol. V, 'Le mouvement socialiste internationale', Quillet: Paris, 1913, pp497-8.
2. Department of History of the KKE Central Committee, *To proto synedrio tou SEKE* (The first congress of the SEKE), KKE Central Committee: Athens, 1982.
3. *Το ΚΚΕ, Επίσημα Κείμενα*, τόμος πρώτος, *1918-1924* (*The KKE, Official Documents*, 1st volume, 1918-1924), Synchroni Epochi: Athens, 1974, pp7-10.
4. *Rizospastis*, 24 October 1920.
5. In its first participation in a nationwide electoral competition, the SEKE(K), with a radical and anti-war electoral program, obtained about 50,000 votes, but failed to elect a deputy in the Parliament (Γεωργαντίδης Χ.Ν., Νικολακόπουλος Ηλίας, 'Η εξέλιξη της εκλογικής δύναμης του ΚΚΕ μεταξύ των δύο πολέμων', *Επιθεώρηση Κοινωνικών Ερευνών* [Ch. N. Georgantidis and Ilias Nikolakopoulos, 'The evolution of the electoral force of the KKE during the interwar period', *The Greek Review of Social Research*], No. 36, 1979, pp448-68). In these elections, which were among the most critical for the Greek in the twentieth century, as they took place during the Greco-Turk War, the expansionist policy of Venizelos was defeated and the majority of electors supported the United Opposition, a conservative coalition of anti-venizelist parties, advocating the stop of the war.
6. *The KKE, Official Documents*, 1st volume, 1918-1924, p160.
7. *Rizospastis*, 24 October 1921.
8. Γ.Α. Γεωργιάδης, 'Η επέτειος της Ρωσσικής Επαναστάσεως' (G.A. Georgiadis, 'The Anniversary of the October Revolution'), *Kommounistiki Epitheorisi*, November 1921, pp369-74.
9. *Rizospastis*, 2 and 3 November 1924.
10. *Rizospastis*, 5 November 1924.
11. *Kommounistiki Epitheorisi*, November 1924.
12. *Rizospastis*, 8 and 10 November 1924.
13. *Eleftheron Vima*, 8 November 1924.
14. In the elections of November 1926, the KKE, presented as 'United Front of Workers, Peasants and Refugees', obtained 4.38 per cent and ten communists were elected members of the Parliament.
15. *Rizospastis*, 7 November 1926.

16. *Rizospastis*, 7 and 9 November 1927.
17. *Rizospastis*, 12 November 1928.
18. *I Pali ton takseon*, 3 November 1931. *I pali ton takseon* (The struggle of the classes) was the official newspaper of the Trotskyist organisation KOMLEA.
19. *O Neos Rizospastis*, 6 November 1931.
20. *Komounistiki Epitheorisi*, No. 21/94, November 1933, p9.
21. Άγγελος Ελεφάντης, *Η επαγγελία της αδύνατης επανάστασης* (Aggelos Elefantis, *The Promise of the Impossible Revolution*), Themelio: Athens, 1979 [1976], pp288-9.
22. *Rizospastis*, 6, 8 and 9 November 1934.
23. *Rizospastis*, 7 November 1934.
24. *Eleftheron Vima*, 8 November 1939.
25. Bernhard H. Bayerlein, Mikhaïl Narinski, Brigitte Studer et Serge Wolikow, *Moscou-Paris-Berlin. Télégrammes chiffrés du Komintern (1939-1941)*, Tallandier: Paris, 2003, pp338-9.
26. *Ibid.*, pp507-8.
27. *Komounistiki Epitheorisi*, November 1942, p112.
28. *Komounistiki Epitheorisi*, November 1943, p415.
29. Ζήσης Ζωγράφος, 'Η 27η επέτειος της Οχτωβριανής επανάστασης' (Zisis Zografos, 'The 27th Anniversary of the October Revolution'), *Komounistiki Epitheorisi*, October – November 1944, pp962-9.
30. Θεοτοκάς Γιώργος, *Τετράδια Ημερολογίου 1939-1953* (George Theotokas, *Notebooks of a diary, 1939-1953*), Estia: Athens, n.d., pp524-5.
31. Φίλιππος Ηλιού, *Ο ελληνικός εμφύλιος πόλεμος. Η εμπλοκή του ΚΚΕ* (Filippos Iliou, *The Greek Civil War. The Embroilment of the ΚΚΕ*), Themelio: Athens, 2004, p44.
32. *Rizospastis*, 8 November 1944.
33. *Rizospastis*, 9 November 1944.
34. *Rizospastis*, 10 and 11 November 1944.
35. Γιώργος Μαργαρίτης, *Ιστορία του ελληνικού εμφυλίου πολέμου, 1946-1949* (Yorgos Margaritis, *A History of the Greek Civil War, 1946-1949*), Volume 1, Vivliorama: Athens, 2000.
36. *Rizospastis*, 6 November 1945.
37. *Rizospastis*, 13 November 1945.
38. *Rizospastis*, 6 November 1945.
39. *Rizospastis*, 8 November 1945.
40. *Eleftheri Ellada*, 7 November 1946.

41. Thanasis D. Sfikas, 'War and Peace in the Strategy of the Greek Communist Party, 1945-1949', *Journal of Cold War Studies*, Vol. 3 No. 3, Fall 2001, pp5-30.
42. *Rizospastis*, 3 November 1946.
43. Σεραφείμ Μάξιμος, 'Τα σοβιέτ και εμείς' (Serafim Maximos, 'Soviets and us'), *Eleftheri Ellada*, 8 November 1946.
44. *Rizospastis*, 5 November 1946.
45. *Rizospastis*, 8 November 1946.
46. *Ergatiki Pali*, 4 November 1946.
47. Γραφείο Διαφώτισης του ΓΑ του ΔΣΕ, 'Χαρακτήρας, μέσα και οργάνωση της διαφώτισης στο Δ.Σ.Ε.' (Bureau of Enlightenment of the General Headquarters of the Democratic Army of Greece, 'Character, Means and Organisation of the Enlightenment in the Democratic Army of Greece'), *Dimokratikos Stratos*, April 1948, pp125-9.
48. Δημήτρης Παλαιολογόπουλος, *Το λαϊκό διδασκαλείο Πελοποννήσου* (Dimitris Paleologopoulos, *The People's School of Teacher Education of Peloponnese*), Nea Skepsi: Athens, 1993, p34.
49. *Dimokratikos Stratos*, January 1948, p3.
50. *Komounistiki Epitheorisi*, November 1947, p486.
51. Contemprary Social History Archives, Democratic Army of Greece, Document 08858.
52. *Dimokratika Nea*, 7 November 1948.
53. Δημήτρης Ν. Κατσής, *Το ημερολόγιο ενός αντάρτη του ΔΣΕ, 1946-1949* (Dimitris N. Katsis, *The Diary of a Partisan of the Democratic Army of Greece, 1946-1949*), Volume 2, Athens, 1992, pp40-1.
54. Βασίλης Μπαρτζιώτας, 'Για τον πολιτικό επίτροπο' (Vassilis Bartziotas, 'About Political Commissars'), *Dimokratikos Stratos*, June 1948, pp189-92.
55. Βασίλης Αποστολόπουλος, *Το χρονικό μιας εποποιίας. Ο ΔΣΕ στη Ρούμελη* (Vasilis Apostolopoulos, *Chronicles of an epic struggle*), Synchroni Epokhi: Athens, 1995 (2nd ed.), p52.
56. *Deltio Idiseon*, 8 November 1948.
57. Paleologopoulos, *op. cit.*, p56.
58. Archives of the KKE, Document 401350.
59. *Dimokratis*, 2 November 1950.

The Mensheviks Commemorate October

André Liebich

The exiled Mensheviks loved commemorations, much as did other European and Russian socialists but, perhaps even more so. When the Bolsheviks came to power, the Mensheviks organised remembrance services for their martyrs, already appeared in processions in 1917 and especially at the second congress of the Comintern in summer 1920, as attested by the numerous photos we have from these occasions.[1] Commemorations were a claim for legitimacy, demonstrating continuity between the past of the socialist tradition and the contested present. The exiled Mensheviks were especially keen to insist upon this continuity in the face of acerbic criticism of their stance from those who had defeated them in Soviet Russia and the latter's sympathisers in the West.[2]

The flagship Menshevik publication, the *Sotsialisticheskii vestnik*, usually translated into English as *The Socialist Herald*, is full of such memorials, tributes, and remembrances. The *Sotsvestnik*, as it was familiarly called, was the organ of the Foreign Delegation of the Russian Social Democratic Labour Party, initially appearing fortnightly, and subsequently monthly and, finally, in the 1960s, annually. Initially, this was one of the two arms of the Menshevik central committee, representing that part of the committee that found itself abroad while the other part resided in Russia. As the party went underground in Russia in the face of persecution, *Sotsvestnik* became its central organ, and continued to proclaim itself as such for some forty years. Between 1921 and 1963, it published almost 800 issues, first in Berlin, then, after 1933, in Paris, and, as of 1940, in New York. To this day, *Sotsvestnik* is considered a reliable source on life in Soviet Russia in the 1920s; reports were published under the heading '*Po Rossii*' ('Around Russia'), as the Mensheviks abroad were supplied with eyewitness material from party members who had stayed behind. Even in later years, the journal earned a deserved reputation as a well-informed and often authoritative commentator on Soviet matters. In the 1920s, it was smuggled into Soviet Russia in various ways, including through the good officers of German and Baltic embassies, who allowed the exiled Mensheviks, as personal friends of West European socialist leaders, to use the diplomatic bag. The number of 2000 copies for that period, cited by the Mensheviks in a circular enquiry of the Labour and Socialist International dating from 1934, is probably exaggerated, and the admission in the same circular that the number had fallen drastically is a sad indication of changing conditions under Soviet rule, especially after the 'Menshevik Trial' of 1931.[3]

Among *Sotsvestnik*'s longstanding contributors and sometime editors were Boris Ivanovitch Nicolaevsky (1887-1966), the famous historian whose name continues to be known through his archives at the Hoover Institution; Solomon Meerovitch Shvarts (1883-1973) a well-known expert on the Soviet economy; David Iulevitch Dallin (1889-1962), later an acclaimed Cold War authority on Soviet foreign policy; Rafael Rein Abramovitch (1880-1963), for many years active in the Socialist International and later a key figure in American interpretations of the Russian Revolution; and Fedor Illitch Dan (1871-1947), a prominent politician in the period of the Provisional Government in Russia in 1917 and later chairman of the Menshevik Party.[4]

The Mensheviks commemorated and commented on one anniversary after another. Early on, they scoffed at Bolshevik attempts to monopolise party history.[5] In 1923, they noted with great pomp the quarter-century anniversary of the Russian Social Democratic Labour Party, emphasising that this was their anniversary as well, even though the Bolsheviks were imprisoning Menshevik Party members and were promoting a movement of former Mensheviks who had slunk over to the Bolshevik side.[6] The following year they noted the sixtieth anniversary of the Socialist International, and drew a direct thread from Marx's International Workingmen's Association to the Labour and Socialist International (LSI). Established in 1923, this was the revived Second International, to which the Mensheviks belonged even as they pointedly rejected the Comintern's claims to continuity with Marx's creation, and having themselves been members of the short-lived Vienna or Two-and-a-Half International.[7] In 1926, under the title 'Pamiatnyi den' internatsionala' (The Memorial Day of the International), they commemorated the tenth anniversary of Friedrich Adler's assassination of the Austro-Hungarian prime minister, Karl von Stürgkh.[8] Adler, the LSI's general secretary, was a close friend and political ally of the Menshevik leaders and the tribute to him was thus personal as well as political. In 1928, Fedor Dan devoted a lengthy article to the tenth anniversary of the (ill-fated) German Revolution, and in 1929, the column *'zagranitsei'* ('Abroad') commemorated the twenty-fifth anniversary of the Königsberg Trial. This was an event involving German and Russian Social Democracy that had attracted attention at the time, but might by now have been considered an obscure chapter in pre-revolutionary activity.[9]

The Mensheviks also marked birthdays: for example, Karl Kautsky's seventy-fifth birthday and Eduard Bernstein's eightieth birthday were duly noted with front page editorials.[10] They commemorated deaths and anniversaries of deaths. *'Piat' let'*

(Five Years) was the title of a 1928 editorial that recalled the demise in 1923 of the exiled party leader Iulii Martov.[11] Also in 1928, almost a whole issue of *Sotsvestnik* was devoted immediately after his death to Pavel Aksel'rod, one of the fathers of the party, while Fedor Dan wrote an article on the tenth anniversary of the death of Georgi Plekhanov, considered the founder of Russian Marxism.[12] Both these leaders had expressed reservations about the party's political orientation in exile, but in death they were honoured as faithful Mensheviks. The tradition of commemorating socialist heroes continued into the 1930s with editorials on the fiftieth anniversary of Karl Marx's death, the tenth anniversary of Martov's death, the seventieth anniversary of the workers' international, and the eightieth birthday of Karl Kautsky.[13] Fedor Dan even published a commemorative article on Alexander Potresov, an early leader of Russian social democracy who had strayed so far from the party line that he had set up a competing Menshevik journal, *Zarya*, and who in flagrant violation of party policy had contributed to Alexander Kerensky's *Dni*.[14] Surprisingly, *Sotsvestnik* also commemorated the tenth anniversary of Lenin's death in 1934, although it did so mostly to revile Stalin.[15]

But with all their enthusiasm for commemoration, the exiled Mensheviks found it difficult to commemorate the October Revolution. The reason behind this lies in party history reaching back to the fateful experience of 1917. In that year, the party was divided into three factions. As well as the defensists, who included Plekhanov, Potresov, and Aksel'rod, there were the revolutionary defensists, notably Irakli Tsereteli (who in exile was to become a Georgian rather than a Russian social democrat) and Fedor Dan, who had what one scholar has called a 'peculiar love-hate attitude' towards the Allies and the war.[16] Finally, there was a minority of Menshevik Internationalists, led by Martov, who were close to the Bolsheviks and called for an all-socialist government. Symbolically, the Internationalists stayed a few hours longer than the other Menshevik factions at the crucial meeting of the Second Congress of Soviets that marked the Bolshevik seizure of power.

In exile, it was the Internationalist line that prevailed at the top. Initially, Martov himself ruled the party in exile, with an iron hand. After his death in 1923, leadership was taken over by Fedor Dan, Martov's brother-in-law through his marriage to Martov's sister, Lidia Osipovna, a revolutionary in her own right.[17] Dan had repented of his revolutionary defensist stand in 1917, and had become a thoroughgoing Martovite Internationalist. In fact, the political programme of the Menshevik Party was known as the 'Martov Line'. However, much of the party, and most party members in Russia, rejected the compromise with Bolshevism that the 'Martov Line' implied and remained firmly grounded in hostility to the Bolshevik order. As a result, *Sotsialisticheskii vestnik* was obliged to cater to two contradictory policies: a 'soft' and compromising Martov Line stance on Bolshevism, and the 'hard', combative and uncompromisingly hostile attitude to the Bolsheviks that was adopted by the party majority.

While in its editorial *Sotsialisticheskii vestnik* celebrated above all the February Revolution, it allowed Dan as editor and party chair to promote the 'Martov Line' in lengthy articles classified as 'feuilletons' and published simultaneously with the editorials.[18] In March 1927, an important date as it heralded the February Revolution's tenth anniversary, Dan bemoaned the stagnation that characterised Soviet Russia and warned that the bourgeoisie was experiencing a rebirth. To be sure, the Russian Revolution had carried out the destructive tasks that stood before it; as he put it, Russians had ceased to be subjects though they were not yet citizens. Drawing upon the authority of a leading Marxist theoretician, Dan cited Kautsky's view that the Russian Revolution was the last bourgeois revolution, and not, as the Communists maintained, the first socialist revolution. While Dan described Kautsky's position as basically correct, he added that, although the revolution was fundamentally bourgeois, it remained a powerful stimulus to socialist proletarian revolution in the more advanced countries, while creating the conditions for quickening development in more backward countries. In short, the objective meaning of the Russian Revolution, in its Bolshevik variant, was to represent a major factor of the world-wide struggle of the proletariat. Though the ten-year cycle of revolution might end with a fascist Bonapartist overturn, and though the chances of a democratic liquidation of the dictatorship were receding, years and perhaps decades would pass before the processes unleashed by the revolutions (in the plural) of 1917 would crystallise in permanent forms, the character of which one could presently only guess. What was nevertheless certain was that one could not return to February – meaning February 1917. The river does not flow backwards, Dan declared. 'Back to February' was a dangerously ambiguous slogan, and it meant ignoring ten years of revolution and restoring social relations that had already been overcome. Dan did not specify who was calling for a return to February but, clearly, his article was a rebuttal of the celebration of the February Revolution implied in the *Sotsvestnik* editorial of the same issue.

Given the attention that the Bolsheviks – and the world of socialism – were lavishing upon the tenth anniversary of the October Revolution, the Mensheviks could not ignore this milestone. One of the most interesting documents that *Sotsvestnik* published on that occasion was a letter from Moscow entitled 'On the Eve of the Tenth Anniversary'. It described the beautification that the capital was undergoing with flags, banners, portraits of leaders everywhere, and with *subbotnik* workers cleaning up the city streets and squares. It also described the special units that were hunting down the homeless and beggars, expelling them from the city. Fearing congestion (overload, stated the article) in Moscow, the authorities were giving instructions to the provinces to limit the number of their delegates and were providing special trains for those Muscovite workers who wanted to go for a three-day holiday into the countryside. At the same time, the 'letter from Moscow' noted that the city was in the throes of a great fear. The inhabitants feared hunger and war, not only external but civil war. In addition to widespread anti-semitism, there was a sharp increase in hostility to foreigners, focused on the well-fed and self-confident visitors who had come to celebrate the revolution's anniversary. Rumours flew that the lack of food was due precisely to the fact that these foreigners were well provided for and even received copious presents 'for the road'. Moreover, as the fear of war was invoked, foreigners were seen as spies come to reconnoitre the terrain. Suspicion towards them prevailed; people declared them worse than 'our own' party authorities. The population had been promised grand celebrations but it was awaiting them with fear.[19]

Sotsvestnik's editorial in this same issue was, as expected, gloomy. Entitled 'The Jubilee Debacle', it invoked the political elimination of much of the Bolshevik 'Old Guard', despite the fact that the Mensheviks had shown little regard for Stalin's present targets, Zinoviev, Kamenev and Trotsky. The latter's defects, notably his refusal to join either party faction before 1917, had earned him almost as much opprobrium among the Mensheviks as it had among the Bolsheviks. Once he became the target of Stalin's wrath and particularly after he had been exiled, the Mensheviks were more inclined to view him in a friendly light, although Trotsky himself continued to shy away from them out of fear of being labelled a 'Menshevik'.[20] *Sotsvestnik*'s 1927 editorial regretted its own illusions, shared by the Bolsheviks themselves, that Bolshevik power would not last ten years. It proclaimed the rebirth of capitalism in Russia which was occurring, not in spite of communism, but through communism, with the activity of managers replacing that of workers in a Thermidorian process of degeneration.[21]

Dan's feuilleton in this issue made some concessions to the sentiments of his party adversaries, not least in entitling his article, the 'Jubilee of the Dictatorship'. He again agreed that the Bolshevik seizure of power was a moment in the bourgeois revolution, that a seizure of power by a proletarian party did not make the revolution proletarian in its social content, and that the October Revolution was the outcome of a conspiracy aided by the party's demagoguery and by utopian illusions among the population. However, he declared openly what his adversaries were reluctant to acknowledge: that by the end of 1917 a significant majority of the Russian working class, disillusioned by the record of the Provisional Government, had gone over to the Bolsheviks. As of now it was the repressive apparatus that ruled in Russia, but the Bolshevik dictatorship was only one stage in the development of a lengthy revolutionary process which had begun in February-March 1917 and which was far from having ended.

In the 1930s, the remnants of the Menshevik party in Russia were exterminated. However, within the party abroad, opposition to the 'Martov Line' grew. On the fifteenth anniversary of the October Revolution in 1932, David Dallin, one of Dan's faithful companions in his adherence to the 'Martov Line', published an ambiguous article that heralded his withdrawal from all party activity (at least until his return to it, as a right-wing Menshevik and Cold Warrior in the very different circumstances of 1940s America).[22] Dallin placed Bolshevism within the grand tradition of those, both bourgeois and socialist, who sought to put an end to Russian backwardness. Russia had now been transformed into a country where there was no capitalism but no hint either of a socialist economy, and where the almost magical 'Europeanisation' of Russia had taken place at the cost of tens of millions of human lives. To be sure, a return to capitalism would be a defeat of socialist ambitions, however utopian these were; but defeat might allow the maintenance of much that was precious in the achievements of the last fifteen years.

Dallin's barely disguised call for giving up on Soviet Russia was a heresy for the proponents of the 'Martov Line', and even for others. Solomon Shvarts's article in the same issue of *Sotsvestnik* provided a much more conventional Menshevik critique of what Bolshevism had done to Russia over its fifteen years in power.[23] In contrast to the fifth and tenth anniversary celebrations, he wrote, there was now complete silence about the social, economic, and political attainments of the working class. This was a reflection of the state-capitalist transformation of the social psyche of the ruling communist bureaucracy. Although Shvarts was painfully wrong in his account of internal migration from the cities to the countryside (at a time of famine peasants were, in fact, fleeing to the cities), his critique of Bolshevik Russia was acceptable to most Mensheviks.

Two years later, in 1934, *Sotsvestnik*'s editorial on the commemoration of the October Revolution confined itself to what would later be known as a 'Kremlinological' analysis of Soviet slogans advanced on that occasion.[24] Was it an accident, the journal asked rhetorically, that Soviet Pioneers were being called upon to 'continue and complete the great work of Lenin' and not 'the great work of Lenin-Stalin' as in previous years? Was it an accident that slogans spoke of the 'banner of Marx-Engels-Lenin' without mentioning Stalin? In any case, the most salient aspect of all the slogans was their apolitical, business-like character, thus confirming Menshevik views about the degeneration of the Revolution and its abandonment of the working class.

The twentieth anniversary of the Bolshevik regime, in 1937, could not pass without notice. It evoked a long article from Dan, still the head of the party but under increasing pressure from opponents of the 'Martov Line'.[25] The article repeated arguments that Dan had made previously and that his critics considered increasingly hollow. Under the heading 'The Twentieth Anniversary of the Dictatorship', Dan made concessions to these critics. The twentieth anniversary of October was not the twentieth anniversary of the revolution, he wrote; it was only the twentieth anniversary of the Bolshevik dictatorship. The great Russian Revolution was born not in October but in February 1917, he declared. At this point, however, Dan reverted to the position he had defended so long. October was but a phase in a single revolutionary process. Moreover, he added, the Bolshevik dictatorship was an inevitable form of revolutionary power. He emphasised here, as he was to do some ten years later in his major work *The Origins of Bolshevism*, the specific Russian conditions that had made Bolshevism possible and even inevitable, criticising those western socialists such as Emile Vandervelde who ignored these conditions.[26] He again acknowledged that the Bolshevik dictatorship was proletarian only in the sense that its bearer was a proletarian party and that it could never be a dictatorship of the proletariat in the Marxist sense. Yes, he conceded, the Bolshevik dictatorship was turning ever more clearly into a brake on Russia's progressive development. It might even have played out its role as a bearer of revolutionary progress, be it in the most barbarian and disfigured form. However, the example of Napoleon showed that a formation which had become counter-revolutionary at home might still play a revolutionary role in the wider world. Not to understand this, to consider October the beginning of the counter-revolution and to call for a 'return to February' – again he did not name those who made such calls – would mean to reject the whole content and course of the revolution, to overlook the great legacy that it had borne and continued to bear, and thus to stand on the side of the counter-revolution.

Within a few years the balance of power within the Menshevik Foreign Delegation moved against Dan and the 'Martov Line'. The terror and the trials of the late 1930s left the Mensheviks uneasy. They had denounced the Bolshevik leadership unrelentingly yet a number of these leaders had once been party comrades and some, like the former Soviet premier Alexeï Rykov, had maintained friendly ties with the exiled Mensheviks whenever they went abroad.[27] Moreover, the Mensheviks were aware that through the trials, Stalin was destroying whatever remained of the old Social Democratic Workers' Party (the RSDLP) in Russia. Decisively for internal party politics, Boris Nicolaevsky, aghast at the suffering of the Russian peasantry, turned against his party leader – although he continued to show him human kindness, and refused to leave Dan on his sickbed as the Germans moved into Paris in June 1940. Within the new power configuration, Rafael Abramovitch became the party chair as Dan and his few faithful supporters first started their own periodical publication – initially *Novyi Mir*, and later *Novyi Put'* – and then, in New York in 1942, left the Foreign Delegation altogether.

That same year, on the occasion of the twenty-fifth anniversary of the February Revolution, *Sotsialisticheskii Vestnik* published an editorial that still incorporated elements of the party's previous policies but struck out in a new direction.[28] The article described February 1917 as Russia's '1848'. This was the revolution that was to open a period of industrial capitalist development, and yet in October of 1917 the long-delayed democratic revolution sought to transform itself into a socialist revolution that was hopelessly premature. Engels had said that there was nothing more dangerous for a revolutionary class than to come to power in conditions which had not ripened for the realisation of its historical tasks. True, it was not the proletariat itself which had attained power but some elements acting in its name. These, moreover, had succeeded, not because of the proletariat's strength, but thanks to the weakness of its adversary, the bourgeoisie, and the backwardness of its ally and potential enemy, the peasantry. Ignoring the Mensheviks' calls for compromise with the peasantry and attention to the needs of the working class, the Bolsheviks had imposed a quarter century of suffering upon the country as they proceeded with the sort of primitive accumulation of capital described by Marx, and erected an all-powerful state apparatus to repress any opposition to their misguided policies. Dan was among those who wanted to believe that the war that was raging in 1942 would be followed by a successful social revolution of the proletariat in the important countries of the world, with the help of the Bolshevik dictatorship in Russia. Glancing obliquely at those who held such views, *Sotsvestnik* rejected this optimistic scenario. For a quarter of a century, the regime in Russia had been a source of weakness, not of strength, for democratic socialism. It would continue to be so in the future.

Dan passed away in 1947, still insisting that Russian conditions explained (and perhaps also justified) Bolshevik excesses, and still hoping that the October Revolution would serve as a spark for the world-wide victory of the proletariat. The Foreign Delegation dissolved in 1951 over arguments concerning the attitude that should be taken towards the new Soviet emigration of displaced persons and Vlasovites, Russians who had fought under German command against the Soviet Union. Disputes over the nature of 'October' receded into the background, as the USSR, now a firmly-established state and superpower, became the main enemy of the western camp. Instead of commenting on the anniversary of the October Revolution, *Sotsvestnik's* editorials now dealt with other matters, such as American and Cold War politics.[29] The journal turned inward, celebrating its own existence and, in a sign of the passage of time, recording obituaries of the party's deserving members.[30] Significantly, on the thirty-seventh anniversary of October in 1954, the editors of the journal did not themselves comment. Instead they chose to reproduce an abbreviated version of the last chapter of the memoir of Mark Vishniak, a prominent socialist revolutionary, and the chapter which specifically dealt with the two revolutions of 1917.[31] This also confirmed the reconciliation, notably in terms of interpretation of the October Revolution, between the exiled Mensheviks and the Socialist Revolutionaries, longtime rivals who had resisted co-operating with each other until the late 1940s.

Sotsvestnik continued to appear into the 1960s but the surviving Mensheviks found other outlets for their writings. Abramovitch published *The Soviet Revolution*, in which he advanced what has been called 'Menshevik history', namely the thesis that tsarist Russia was already experiencing robust capitalist development in the last years of the *ancien régime* and was moving quickly towards industrialisation and democracy.[32] In fact, this did not correspond to the previously established views of either left- or right-wing Mensheviks. In part for that reason, but also for many other reasons, Lidia Osipovna, by then the grand old lady of Menshevism and still generous, as always, was restrained in her assessment of the book; 'better than [she] had feared', was all she could bring herself about to say of it.[33] Dallin and Nicolaevsky were active in various anti-Soviet Cold War organisations. The former became a highly respected pundit on Soviet affairs, expressing his views in numerous books and articles.[34] The latter continued his historical work but could not resist re-entering the fray of Menshevik politics. Somewhat cryptically, he stated, in 1950, that the February Revolution was 'accidental' but that the October Revolution was 'inevitable'.[35] He did not elaborate on what he meant.

Sotsialisticheskii vestnik held a record as the longest surviving socialist émigré journal, probably not only among Russians but among émigrés in general. For many years the exiled Mensheviks saw their mission as that of holding the banner of Russian democratic socialism high, as incarnating the belief that democratic socialism might yet return to Russia. Their faith was sorely tried as they moved from trust in a '*spusk po tormozakh*', a belief in an internal change in Russia, a slowing down of the revolution, to a forlorn hope that change might be induced from the outside in the conditions of the Cold War. Nicolaevsky's cryptic statement about the two revolutions of 1917 suggests that he saw the birth of a bourgeois-democratic order in Russia as a hope, but the Bolshevik or 'maximalist' revolution that followed as an inevitability. But then, Nicolaevsky was a contrarian and he may have been only provoking his comrades or succumbing to a moment of pessimism. He was not expressing what has remained as the heritage of the exiled Mensheviks.

NOTES

1. André Liebich and Svetlana Yakimovich (eds), *From Communism to Anti-Communism: Photographs from the Boris Souvarine Collection at the Graduate Institute, Geneva*, elivres de l'Institut/6, Geneva: Graduate Institute Publications, 2016, books.openedition.org/iheid/6440, 31 July 2017.
2. André Liebich (with Albert Nenarokov), 'Kak rossiiskie sotsialdemokraty otmetili svoi serebrianyi iubilei', in *Istoricheskaia Pamiat' i obschchestvo v Rossiiskoi imperii i sovetskom Soiuze (konets XIX – nachalo XX veka)*, mezhdunarodnyi kollokvium, nauchnye doklady, Saint Petersburg, 25-28 June 2007, pp164-76.
3. Fragebogen über die Verhältnisse der S.A.I angeschlossenen illegalen Parteien, 5 November 1934, Rossiiskii tsentr khraneniia i izucheniia dokumentov noveishei istorii, f. 480, op. 3, p40.
4. The party in exile is the subject of my monograph, *From the Other Shore: Russian Social Democracy after 1921*, Harvard University Press: Cambridge, MA, 1997. Spellings of proper names differ according to circumstances; thus Nikolaevskii, Shwartz, Abramowitch as well as the transliterations given in the text.
5. See 'Kak rossiiskie sotsial-demokraty otmetili svoi serebrianyi iubilei'.

6. 'Chetvert' veka' [editorial], *Sotsialisticheskii vestnik (SV)*, No. 5-6 (51-52), 16 March 1923.
7. '60-letie Internatsionala' [editorial], *SV*, No. 19 (89), 8 October 1924. The classic work on the Vienna International is still Andre P. Donneur, *Histoire de l'Union de partis socialistes pour l'action international (1920-1923)*, Librairie de l'Université laurentienne: Sudbury, 1967.
8. 'Pamiatnyi den' internatsionala' [editorial], *SV*, No. 138 (20), 16 October 1926.
9. '25 letie kenigbergskogo protsessa [za granitsei]', *SV*, No. 292 (12), 15 June 1929. The trial is discussed in Bruno Naarden, *Socialist Europe and Revolutionary Russia: Perception and Prejudice, 1848-1923*, Cambridge University Press: Cambridge, 2002, p149.
10. 'K 75-letiiu Karla Kaustskogo', *SV*, No. 209 (19), 10 October 1929, and 'K 80-letiiu Eduarda Bernshteina', *SV*, No. 215 (1), 1 January 1930.
11. F. Dan, 'Piat' let', *SV*, No, 173 (7), 4 April 1928. Israel Getzler, *Martov: A Political Biography of a Russian Social Democrat*, Cambridge University Press: Cambridge, 1963, is still the indispensable biography.
12. On Aksel'rod's death, *SV*, No. 174/175 (8/9), 3 May 1928. F. Dan, 'Ku desiatiletiiu smerti G. B. Plekhanova' [editorial], *SV*, No. 187 (21), 14 November 1928. Classic biographies are Abraham Ascher, *Paul Axelrod and the Development of Marxism*, Harvard University Press: Cambridge, MA, 1972, and Samuel H. Baron, *Plekhanov: the Father of Russian Marxism*, Stanford University Press: Stanford, 1963.
13. 'K 50 letiiu smerti Karl Marksa', *SV*, No. 289/290 (4/5), 4 March 1933; '70 letiie rabochego internatsionala' and 'K 80 letiiu Kautskogo', *SV*, No. 328 (19), 10 October 1934.
14. F. Dan, 'Pamiati Potresova', *SV*, No. 323 (14), 25 June 1934. Note that this issue is dated a few weeks before Potresov's death though in all likelihood it appeared later.
15. 'Cherez desiat' let' [editorial], *SV*, No. 311 (2), 26 January 1934.
16. Rex A. Wade, *The Russian Search for Peace, February-October 1917*, Stanford University Press: Stanford, 1969, p145.
17. A biography of Lidia Osipovna [Dan] is S. Jebrak, *Mit dem Blick nach Russland. Lydia Cederbaum (1878-1963): eine jüdische Sozialdemokratin im lebenslangem Exil*, Dietz: Bonn, 2006. See especially Boris Sapir (ed.), *Iz Arkhiva L.O. Dan*, Stichting Beheer IISG: Amsterdam, 1987.
18. 'K iubileiu revoliutsii' [editorial], and F. Dan, 'Desiat' let' [feuilleton], *SV*, No. 147/148 (5/6), 12 March 1927.

19. 'Nakanune desiatiletiia [pis'mo iz moskvy]', *SV,* No. 163/164 (21/22), 10 November 1927.
20. The one amiable connection between Trotsky and the Mensheviks was an academic one through Trotsky's son, Leon Sedov, who gave some of his father's papers for safekeeping to the Menshevik historian, Boris Nicolaevsky, in Paris in the 1930s. Even this expression of confidence was sorely tried when Trotsky's papers were stolen from Nicolaevsky's office in 1936. See Andre Liebich, 'From Archives to Politics: Boris Nicolaevsky in Paris (1933-1940)', in Tom Kilton and Ceres Birkhead (eds), *Migrations in Society, Culture, and the Library,* Proceedings of the ACRL Western European Studies Section Conference, Paris, France, 22-26 March 2004, ACRL: Chicago, 2005, pp38-51.
21. 'iubileinyi razgrom' [editorial], *SV,* No. 163/164 (21/22), 10 November 1927.
22. D. Dalin, 'Iubilei', *SV,* No. 282 (21), 12 November 1932.
23. S. Shvarts, 'O chem molchali v iubileinye dni?', *SV,* No. 282 (21), 12 November 1932.
24. 'Oktiabrskie lozungi' [editorial], *SV,* No. 330 (21), 10 November 1934.
25. F. Dan, Dvadtsatiletie diktatury', *SV,* No. 400 (20), 20 November 1937.
26. F. Dan, *Proiskhozhdenie bol'shevizma : k istorii demokraticheskikh i sotsialisticheskikh idei v Rossii posle osvobozhdeniia krest'ian,* Novaia Demokratiia: New York, 1946. In English, Theodore Dan, *The Origins of Bolshevism,* edited and translated from the Russian by Joel Carmichael, with a preface by Leonard Schapiro, Schocken Books: New York, 1964.
27. Alexeï Rykov was Boris Nicolaevsky's brother in law. The case of Nikolai Bukharin's dealings in Paris with Fedor Dan have been the subject of considerable polemic. See Andre Liebich, 'I Am the Last. Memories of Bukharin in Paris', *Slavic Review,* Vol. 51 No. 4, 1992, pp767-781.
28. 'Russkaia revoliutsiia i rabochii klass (k 25-letiiu fevral'skoi revoliutsii)' [editorial], *SV,* No. 493 (5), 14 March 1942.
29. 'Bolezn' Prezidenta Eizenhauera' [editorial], *SV,* No. 687 (10), October 1955; 'Plan Marshalla dlia Azii', *SV,* No. 676 (11), November 1954.
30. For example, 'Dvadtstipiatiletiie Sotsialisticheskogo vesnika [1921-1946]', *SV,* No. 581 (1), 18 January 1946; Daniel Bell, 'At a Vecherinka [letter from New York]', *Encounter,* No. 7, July 1956,

pp65-68, 'Nekrologi'; *Tables de la Revue russe. Le Messager Socialiste 1921-1963 : Le Messager Socialiste, recueil: 1964-1965*, published by La Bibliothèque russe Tourguénev, La Bibliothèque de documentation internationale contemporaine and Alexandre Lande, Institut d'études slaves: Paris, 1992, pp205-209.

31. M. Vishniak, 'Fevral' i oktiabr', *SV*, No. 676 (11), November 1954. The chapter's heading introduced by the editors is '37 let bol'shevizma' and the chapter also includes an article by Boris Nicolaevsky entitled, 'Novaia rabota po istorii kommunizma'.

32. R. Raphael Abramovitch, *The Soviet Revolution, 1917-1939*, introduction by Sidney Hook, International University Press: New York, 1962.

33. L. O. Dan to Volskii, 8 August 1960, Volsky Collection, Hoover Institution Archives, Stanford.

34. See André Liebich, 'Mensheviks Wage the Cold War', *Journal of Contemporary History*, Vol. 30 No. 2, 1995, pp247-263.

35. Nikolaevskii to Volskii, 23 February 1950, Volsky Collection, Hoover Institution Archives, Stanford.

The Echoes of the Echoes: Reflecting the International Commemoration of the October Revolution in the Newspaper *Pravda*, 1918-91

Stephan Rindlisbacher

'It is necessary (for purely political reasons) to demonstrate to the diplomats and to members of the Communist International the strength of the Republic and the faith the masses of workers have in Soviet power'.[1] With these words, Leon Trotsky emphasised in 1920 the importance of the October commemoration as a showpiece of the Soviet regime and of its aspirations to trigger world revolution. However, in practice, this international recognition for the October commemorations became more and more a tool in the hand of the ruling communist party to legitimate its leading role to the Soviet public.

Employing Pierre Nora's concept of the *lieu de mémoire*, this article shows how the October Revolution from 1918 was the central 'realm of memory' in the Soviet politics of memory. The commemoration of 7 November was the essential event by which the Soviet communist party sought to legitimise both its own domestic authority on the one hand and its leading position in the international communist movement on the other. Nevertheless, the marking of Red October was also in constant competition with 1 May, already established internationally as the commemoration day of the workers' movement, and subsequently with the celebration in the USSR of 9 May as Victory Day following its institutionalisation in 1965. While 1 May had a clearly civilian character, and 9 May a military one, the commemoration of Red October was, with its civilian and military dimensions, a hybrid. Together these three main Soviet mass rituals and their reception were intended to implement socialist norms and values in society. The parades in Moscow's Red Square were at the centre, radiating to the parades in the capitals of the Soviet republics and the provincial towns. According to Malte Rolf, the Soviet regime was, with its longing for mass spectacle, a 'dictatorship of staging' (*Inszenierungsdiktatur*).[2]

In the following pages I consider the function of the commemorations abroad for the Soviet self-image. Was the object to renew the revolutionary aspirations within and beyond the Soviet state, or was it conversely to emphasise the latter's standing in the world? To answer these questions, I will analyse how the reception of the Red October abroad was reported in *Pravda*, the newspaper of the Russian (from 1925 All-Union) Communist Party (RCP, AUCP, then CPSU). In Pierre Nora's concept of the *lieu de mémoire*, it is not the description of the past as such that is the focus, but the way in which societies produce and reproduce their past in the present: in other words, how certain elements of the past can serve as symbols of the present order.[3]

Red October was commemorated in order to produce a sense of collective identity in defining the present and constructing the future of Soviet power. Before, during and after the annual festivities, the Soviet media reported on the event's reception abroad as well as nationally. Every year, *Pravda* devoted considerable space to these reports, and it is these which, from 1918 until the USSR's collapse in 1991 (and beyond), provide the basis for my analysis. Its focus is on the forms of commemoration abroad and their function in the official Soviet politics of memory.

From the first year of the revolution, the Bolsheviks had eliminated pluralism, not only in the field of politics, but also in the media.[4] *Pravda*, along with the Soviet daily *Izvestiia*, was the main print newspaper in the Soviet state. Companies, administrative branches, and party organisations had to subscribe, and newspaper stands sold it for a low price. *Pravda*'s messages potentially reached every citizen. Although its name meant 'truth', *Pravda* mirrored the changing and often contradictory lines of the communist party. It stood at the centre of the Soviet news system and was more closely linked with the party leadership than either *Izvestiia* or any other newspaper. Moreover, *Pravda*'s assessments provided a normative framework for Soviet public discourse and for other journalists.[5] The way the echoes were reported reflected the self-image of the regime and, along with the celebrations themselves, demonstrated its standing in the world as well as the projected universality of its ideology.[6]

From the end of the civil war in 1921, the Soviet state was in a distinctive international position. Although on the one hand, it established regular diplomatic relations with 'capitalist states', it also tried to revolutionise their 'bourgeois order', with the Comintern functioning between 1919 and 1943 as the main actor in this field.[7] This twofold policy was clearly reflected in the reporting of the October commemorations. From 1920 onwards, *Pravda* covered meetings and demonstrations abroad, but it also reported on receptions in Soviet embassies around the world and printed congratulatory telegrams from foreign heads of state. In this period of Soviet history, there was a turn from world revolutionary aspirations to a politics of national interest, which can be identified in turning points like Stalin's 'socialism in one country' slogan of 1924 or the Comintern's dissolution in 1943.[8]

Reading the commemoration reports from abroad in *Pravda*, I demonstrate in this chapter that the main turning point can be dated to 1938 and Stalin's shifting of ideological emphasis from the international narrative to one of 'socialism in one country'. This new interpretation of the party's ideological orientation was intended to preserve Stalin's authority and secure the achievements of the forced industrialisation and collectivisation.[9] The policy also opened the way to the August 1939 non-aggression pact with Nazi-Germany, with its secret protocol dividing Eastern Europe.[10] *Pravda* presented the Soviet state as a respected player in world politics, among the other great powers; the idea of Red October as the trigger of a universal revolution was now part of Soviet past. In arguing this thesis through the use of selected examples, I will sketch the echoes of the echoes from abroad in three parts: first, the revolutionary commemoration until 1938; secondly, the reorientation during the Second World War; and finally, the state-centred commemoration after 1945.

REVOLUTIONARY COMMEMORATION 1918-38

7 November 1918 marked the beginning of the annual commemorations of Red October in Soviet Russia. The first commemoration meeting took place at the Theatre Square, not far from the Kremlin. Lenin was there to unveil a statue of Marx and Engels, and as Soviet media began to push the new public holiday, *Pravda* published a front-page picture of this event. The report was joined with an article on the ongoing revolutionary events in Germany.[11] World revolution seemed at this point to be an imminent prospect. The Austro-Hungarian monarchy collapsed, and in Germany the Kaiser abdicated. Leftist parties came to power, as soldiers and workers formed councils, following the Russian example. These revolutionary hopes, however, were soon disappointed; and whereas communist movements had failed to gain power in the West, on 7 November 1919, Trotsky's troops could celebrate their victories in the civil war and commemorate the second anniversary

of Red October. For the first time, the commemoration event took place in Red Square.

As the prospect of an immediate revolution outside Soviet Russia vanished into thin air, Lenin's government had to find a *modus vivendi* with the 'bourgeois' states. The world revolution had for the time being to be postponed, and in November 1920, *Pravda* published its first reports of commemorative demonstrations and meetings abroad. The front page featured a report from Berlin:

> [On] 7 November, communist and independent leftists organised demonstrations in different parts of the town, commemorating the Russian Revolution. The main meeting took place in the Lustgarten, where ... many people came together. ... Soviet stars, the Soviet flag and other emblems were visible. There was no disruption.[12]

Taking the 7 November as the occasion, the temporary occupation of public space by Soviet symbols and flags aimed to keep revolutionary hopes alive and to institutionalise Red October as a binding *lieu de mémoire* for the communist movement all over the world.

The fifth anniversary of the October Revolution, in 1922, coincided with the fourth congress of the Comintern and was a particular focus for celebration.[13] The head of the Comintern, Grigori Zinoviev declared: 'The Russian proletarian revolution ... lives in the hearts of all workers over the world, it has delivered to them an example and calls them to new heroic deeds and gives them hope and a leading star'.[14] Lenin also stressed before the Comintern that the workers of the world 'should learn to understand the experience of the Russian Revolution.[15] However, the Soviet state had to balance its revolutionary aspirations with realpolitik. This is particularly visible in the congratulatory telegram of Mustafa Kemal (later Atatürk) printed on 14 November 1922. The leader of the Turkish nationalists and, at that time, a close ally of the Soviet state, Kemal underlined in his message his warmest feelings for the October Revolution: 'I send my most honest congratulations on the occasion of the fifth anniversary of the historical day, when the Russian people took the flag of the revolution, overthrew the old regime and built a new era in the history of Russia'.[16] For Mustafa Kemal, Red October was a Russian and not an international holiday. However, in the 1920s, the publication of such congratulatory telegrams occurred quite rarely.

In the years after Lenin's death in 1924, the commemorative procedure in Moscow became increasingly elaborate and canonical in character. *Pravda* developed a special format for the commemorations of Red October. Next to reports and pictures from the parade in Red Square, there were always notes from abroad combined with those from the different regions of the Soviet Union. In this way, the Soviet public could read that the ruling party was a part of a globally recognised movement. On *Pravda*'s front pages, Soviet citizens were informed of how 'East and West celebrate Red October'. Meetings and demonstrations were organised by the communist parties in Germany, France, the USA, and Britain, but also in China, as well as by the few Soviet embassies.[17]

From the beginning of the 1930s, Stalin's presence grew ever larger in Soviet public space, and this was also reflected in the printing press and particularly in *Pravda*'s anniversary issues.[18] With Stalin's ascension to absolute power and the end of the New Economic Policy, there was a shift in the way the commemorations abroad were perceived. Reports of slogans like 'we are greeting the October Revolution as a harbinger of the world revolution' were now supplemented, but not totally replaced, by slogans like 'we will defend the Soviet Union up to the last drop of our blood'.[19] In the years of Stalinist repression, the notes about the echoes from abroad were placed on the last pages of the party newspaper, while party leaders' speeches and reports on successful industrialisation and the achievements of Stakhanovite workers took the front pages.[20] Reporting on celebrations of the 'proletarian revolution' abroad, *Pravda* developed its own symbolic hierarchy in relation to current communist policy. In 1936, for instance, the celebrations in Madrid and the Spanish republic's revolutionary effort in the war against the Francists were at the centre.[21] However, in this year, we can also observe a certain shift; among the notes about the celebrations abroad, there was a short list of telegrams received by the Soviet government from foreign heads of state. Among them were the shahs of Persia and Afghanistan, as well as Kemal Atatürk (again), the president of the Spanish republic and the president of the USA – Franklin D. Roosevelt.[22] In the years that followed, congratulatory messages such as these featured more and more in *Pravda*'s coverage.

IN THE SHADOW OF WAR

These gradual shifts away from internationalism, and from multinationalism in Soviet internal policy, became clearly visible in the *Short Course on the History of the communist party* in 1938. With Stalin's approval, this book dogmatically defined the history of the Bolshevik Party in public discourse. As such, Stalin's main goal was now to further the monolithic state and its goal of building socialism in one country. Only lip service was paid to internationalism.[23] The deal with Hitler in August 1939 seemed to be one of the consequences of this. *Pravda* had to follow the new line, and it dramatically reduced the prominence of internationalism and proletarian solidarity. Hence, in November 1939, it focused on diplomatic receptions in neutral and pro-axis states commemorating Red October. In Berlin there was a celebration at the Soviet embassy in which Hermann Göring and Joachim von Ribbentrop took part.[24] Reports of October demonstrations or meetings abroad virtually disappeared in this year, the Baltic states and Romania alone were excepted.[25] These were exactly the states which, according to the secret protocol to the pact with Germany, belonged to the Soviet sphere of influence.[26] These reports praised the achievements of the Soviet regime since 1917, and stressed the good and friendly relations that existed between them. Just half a year later, the Baltic states and Bessarabia were occupied by the Red Army and annexed to the Soviet Union.[27] But on the occasion of the October Revolution commemorations, there were still in 1939 no congratulatory telegrams printed from the newly allied German and Italian governments. Ideological differences thus still persisted.

Ironically, Hitler's National Socialists had one of their most important commemoration days, the Memorial Day for the martyrs of the movement, on 9 November, two days after the commemoration of Red October.[28] On 8 November 1939, Georg Eiser, an antifascist resistance fighter, working alone, tried to assassinate Hitler during a ceremony at the Bürgerbräukeller in Munich. In the days that followed, the Soviet government expressed its deepest sympathies for the victims of the attack. Alongside reports of the October commemoration, *Pravda* even printed in full Hitler's speech at the Bürgerbäukeller, in which he underlined Germany's longing for peace, but also his determination never to surrender to the 'English warmongers'.[29]

The ostensibly cordial relations with Hitler did not even last two years. Following the German invasion of the USSR in June 1941, the Soviet Union had to re-establish good relations with the west. Nevertheless, the ways of reporting in *Pravda* changed only in content, not in their basic character. From November 1941, congratulatory telegrams were again made public. Amongst the well-wishers were 'bourgeois' politicians like Richard Hanson, leader of the conservative faction in the Canadian parliament, who wrote: 'Concerning the anniversary of the Soviet Union's foundation, all Canadians pay tribute to the courageous Soviet soldiers and workers. They have gained the respect of the whole world. In this moment, they fight ... for the preservation of civilisation'.[30] In order to mobilise all forces for the defeat of Nazi Germany, former ideological differences seemed to be erased.[31]

In full public views, the non-communist well-wishers for the most part clearly identified Red October as a national, not an international, holiday. For instance, in November 1945, after the Allied victory over the Axis powers, US President Harry Truman underlined in his telegram:

> On the occasion of the national holiday of the Soviet Union, I am delighted to send ... the Soviet people my best wishes and the compliments of the people of the United States of America.
> ... The coming years give us the unprecedented possibility of peaceful progress and the betterment of the destiny of the common man.[32]

The peaceful future described by Truman nevertheless failed to be realised. The Soviet Union and the USA were in an escalating conflict, which finally led to the division of the world into two competing blocs and established the era of the Cold War.

RED OCTOBER AS PART OF SOVIET HISTORY

Beginning in the 1940s and becoming increasingly ritualised in the 1950s, congratulatory telegrams were a hallmark of *Pravda*'s coverage following 7 November. Focusing on support from the allied Eastern European regimes and non-aligned states, in these years the newspaper established a fixed procedure of reporting from abroad. Beginning on 7 November, congratulatory telegrams from foreign governments, communist parties, and political activists were published in each edition until 12 or 13 November. In this way, *Pravda* could demonstrate for a Soviet audience the significance of the Soviet state and Red October to the whole world. To borrow Peter Burke's expression, it performed the Soviet regime as a recognised superpower as well as a leader of 'progressive mankind'.[33] Among the telegrams received were those from allied communist regimes in Europe and Asia (and later also in Africa and the Americas) as well as the 'capitalist states'. The former, along with those from communist parties all over the world, were usually much longer and more ideologically standardised than those of non-communist origin. Over the years, there also developed a clear hierarchy, with the telegrams of the communist allies printed first, and then those from the 'capitalist governments'.

In 1956, in the immediate aftermath of the Hungarian uprising, 'western' governments refused to send congratulatory telegrams. The Soviet regime had clearly demonstrated in Hungary that there was no way for its allies in Eastern Europe to leave the Soviet bloc.[34] In these troubling times, the telegram of Wilhelm Pieck, president of the German Democratic Republic, was published immediately after Mao Zedong's, the leader of what as yet remained the USSR's most powerful ally. Pieck particularly underlined the friendly relations between the GDR and the Soviet Union:

> On the occasion of the thirty-ninth anniversary of the Great Socialist October Revolution the workers of the German Democratic Republic are asserting again to the Soviet peoples their brotherly close relation. The states of the socialist camp are acting hand in hand, led by the spirit of proletarian internationalism. Their friendship and cooperation serves to build socialism for the workers and to defend and preserve peace for the whole mankind.[35]

In his telegram, Wilhelm Pieck presupposed the existence of two competing blocs. He confined the construction of socialism to the Soviet camp, whereas he suggested that peace ought to be a goal for the entire world. Socialism, according to statements like this, was now not a universalist project, but one of the Eastern bloc alone. For this common purpose, the bloc had to hold together and preserve the status quo, if necessary by force.

However, over the course of the next year, the anti-Soviet mood in the western countries calmed. In October 1957, the Soviets experienced a seminal technological success with the launch of Sputnik, the world's first artificial satellite. Now they would be able to carry an atomic bomb to virtually every point on earth and thereby had the potential to attack the USA directly.[36] The latter were no longer secured by the two oceans, which is also why missiles were proudly presented during the October parade and in *Pravda* in 1957.[37] Just as they had prior to 1956, the Soviet government received and *Pravda* once more published congratulatory telegrams from all over the world. Before the Soviet public, their political system was presented as a model for the USSR's allies that was also respected by the enemy capitalist states.

The telegram from Hans Streuli, president of the Swiss Confederation, illustrates the challenges western governments had to overcome in their dealings with the Soviets. Anti-Soviet sentiment in Switzerland was particularly impassioned following the Soviet intervention in Hungary.[38] Streuli therefore had to find a balance between this strong anti-communist mood and diplomatic necessities. He finally did so by congratulating Kliment Voroshilov, the nominal head of the Soviet state, in the briefest fashion possible, without further diplomatic ornaments: 'I have the honour to send you ... on the occasion of the national holiday the greetings of the Swiss government and its best wishes for you ... and the Soviet people'. In focussing on the national character of the October Revolution, Streuli was in line with other non-

Soviet countries, whereas the communist parties or satellite states pointed to its 'proletarian' meaning and its model character for the entire world.[39]

Virtually at the end of this annual flood of telegrams, there were also congratulations from liberation movements. Yasser Arafat's telegrams in the name of the Palestinian Liberation Organisation were from the 1970s regularly at the bottom of the table.[40] In his greetings the Palestinian leader particularly remembered Lenin's promise to all nations of independence and self-determination: 'The great October Revolution and its glorious anniversaries inspire the suppressed nations, which are in a just war against imperialism, Zionism, and racism – the powers which want to enslave, suppress, exploit the nations and plunder their wealth'.[41] But in *Pravda*'s perception, claims to realise Lenin's promises took second place to daily international affairs; revolutionary liberation movements had to bide their time.

Monotonous pages of reprinted telegrams were indicative of the handling of Red October as a whole: like the Red Square parades, this became repetitive, predictable, and, in the very end, outmoded and boring. It was only in the pages following the telegrams that notes from celebrations abroad were reported. Again a clear hierarchy emerged, focusing first on the countries of the Warsaw Pact and China (until the split in the mid-1960s), and only then on reports from Italy, France, or Mexico. The number of the participants in meetings and demonstrations in non-communist countries was usually not indicated.

These tendencies were leading to what I would call a historicisation of Red October. The symbol of the October Revolution was no longer a *lieu de mémoire* for revolutionary politics in the present, rather it was one for the divided status quo. Hence, *Pravda* presented the idea of world revolution as part of the Soviet past. For instance, in 1983, at a climax of the Cold War, *Pravda* published a series of reports on how Red October was celebrated abroad under the title 'October around the planet'.⁴² In Sofia, Kabul, Lima, Amman, and Mexico City, demonstrations and meetings were organised. There was also a note about a celebration in Dundee in Scotland where the local communist party secretary described Red October as 'the most important event in the twentieth century. It changed the direction of world history ... and opened perspectives for social and economic progress to the whole of mankind'.⁴³ In other words, if Red October contributed to world history, it was now as part of the past, not of the present or the future. This report was accompanied by a caricature in which Soviet power acted as protector of 'world peace'. In this caricature, the cruiser *Aurora* had frightened the capitalists and monarchists in 1917. In 1983, however, the futuristic Soviet city-fortress (which was still under construction) would guarantee peace and resist the threats of the 'cowboys' who were planning a new crusade. This was a clear allusion to the policy of the Reagan administration.

However, two days later *Pravda* also published Ronald Reagan's own telegram of greetings, placed between those from the king of Norway and those from the president of Burma. Though *Pravda* showed its depreciation of the president of the rival superpower by placing him between second- and third-order heads of state, his message to the Soviet people was still made public. After the usual congratulations, the message underlined that the USA desired to continue its efforts for world peace, 'which should be based on the respect for international law'. This was a clear allusion to Soviet policy in Afghanistan.⁴⁴

This deadlock of repetitive and uniform reports from abroad was lifted only with the beginning of perestroika. In 1987, leaders of socialist and communist parties and movements all over the world had the chance to express their views about the seventieth anniversary of October.⁴⁵ Politicians like Fuad Mursi, a leading member of the Marxist Egyptian National Progressive Unionist

Party, could express their delight with Mikhail Gorbachev's new policy: 'The new way of thinking in the USSR with the goal of reconstruction [*perestroika*] is not simply a continuation of the October Revolution, but an evolution and extension of its basic ideas'.[46] Mursi saw the possibility of ending the threat of a nuclear war. Under the aegis of the United Nations, conflicts in the Middle East could now be solved, and US imperialist interference, which drove the region into chaos, thereby terminated.

Gorbachev's policy raised short-lived hopes of progress and peace in the third world, and of transparency as well as reconstruction inside the USSR. However, these hopes were rapidly to be disappointed: the political crisis of the Soviet state became acute, and both the party and its ideology were losing their authority. This was also reflected in *Pravda*'s reports after 7 November. Beginning in 1988, congratulatory telegrams were no longer cited in full, but compiled together. Reports on celebrations abroad virtually disappeared, and in 1990 events in Havana, Hanoi, Kabul, Luanda, and Buenos Aires were alone mentioned.[47] In November 1991, after the failed August putsch, the meaning of the commemorations of Red October in the Soviet Union was completely in jeopardy. There was no longer an official parade in Red Square and the echoes from abroad reported in the former party newspaper vanished almost completely.

POST SCRIPTUM

In 1965, 9 May – Victory Day – was institutionalised as a Soviet national holiday. It soon became the most important competitor to Red October in the Soviet commemorative calendar. In contrast to the October Revolution, it was clearly connected to the memories and experiences of the people. In recalling the war against Germany and the uncountable losses on the Soviet side, as well as a final victory, it was not connected to a specific party or ideology.

Victory Day was and remains a *lieu de mémoire* much more closely connected to Soviet family histories and oral tradition than Red October ever could have been, since it was the coup d'état of a rather small group, locally restricted to Petrograd and Moscow. This is also why the Victory Day holiday survived in almost all former Soviet republics. Particularly in Russia, Victory Day is now the core part of the official politics of memory.[48]

In the calendar of the Communist Party of the Russian Federation (CPRF), the successor of the CPSU, the anniversary of the October Revolution is still an outstanding date. In the years after 1991, the party regularly organised Red Square demonstrations on 7 November, and *Pravda*, now the organ of the 'loyalist' opposition party, faithfully described these acts of factional commemoration. In 2007, for example, it reported a meeting of several communist parties commemorating the ninetieth anniversary in Minsk.[49] There, in Belarus, Red October was re-established after Aleksandr Lukashenko's ascension in 1994. *Pravda* and Lukashenko still declare that Red October was a moment of social progress, and the collapse of the Soviet Union a global catastrophe.[50] But outside the Russian-speaking orbit, except for certain Leninist splinter groups, Red October has lost almost all its meaning as a *lieu de mémoire* for actual political practice.

Writing this article in November 2016 in Moscow, I observed a contest for public space in the very centre of the city. Since 2011, Vladimir Putin's regime had begun to occupy Red Square on 7 November with a competing commemoration meeting. Putin's advisers found a dexterous solution to get rid of the communist commemoration. Officially, there is now a commemoration of the October Parade of 7 November 1941, when Moscow was almost under siege by the Germans, and Soviet troops were sent directly from the parade to the front. As a result of this Matryoshka-style commemoration of a commemoration, the CPRF was forced to meet at Theatre Square 200 metres away from Red Square. Ironically, the Russian communists met precisely on the spot where the very first commemoration of the October Revolution took place ninety-eight years earlier.

NOTES

1. Telegram from Trotsky to the CC of the PCR, 1920, Russian State Archive of Socio-Political History (RGASPI), f. 17, op. 60, d. 163, l. 1.
2. Malte Rolf, *Das sowjetische Massenfest*, Hamburger Edition: Hamburg, 2006, pp7-8, pp337-42; Christel Lane, *The Rites of Rulers. Ritual in Industrial Society: The Soviet Case*, Cambridge University Press: Cambridge, 1981, pp24-5; Vladimir Glebkin, *Ritual v sovetskioi kul'ture*, Janus-K: Moscow, 1998, pp74-7.
3. Pierre Nora, 'Entre mémoire et histoire. La problématique des lieux', in Pierre Nora (ed.), *Les lieux de mémoire*, Gallimard: Paris, 1984, ppXXXIV-XXXV. On the symolical use of the past in the German context, see Aleida Assmann, *Der lange Schatten der Vergangenheit: Erinnerungskultur und Geschichtspolitik*, Beck: Munich, 2006, pp274-5; Manuel Becker, *Geschichtspolitik in der 'Berliner Republik': Konzeptionen und Kontroversen*, Springer: Wiesbaden, 2013, pp129-36.
4. Jeffrey Brooks, *Thank you, Comrade Stalin! Soviet Public Culture from Revolution to Cold War*, Princeton University Press: Princeton, 2000, pp3-4.
5. *Ibid.*, ppXVIII-XIX.
6. Rolf, *op. cit.*, p344.
7. Heiko Haumann, 'Vom Bürgerkrieg zum kollektiven Sicherheitssystem: Selbstbehauptung des neuen Staates', in Gottfried Schramm (ed.), *Handbuch der Geschichte Russlands: 1856-1945 von den autokratischen Reformen zum Sowjetstaat* (3 vol., 1 subvol.), Anton Hiersemann: Stuttgart, 1983, pp638-70; Brigitte Studer, *The Transnational World of the Cominternians*, Palgrave Macmillan: Basingstoke, 2015; Hermann Weber, Jakov Drabkin and Bernhard H. Bayerlein (eds), *Deutschland, Russland, Komintern*, 2 vol., De Gruyter: Berlin, 2014-2015.
8. Gleb Albert, "Esteemed Comintern!' The Communist International

and World-Revolutionary Charisma in Early Soviet Society', *Twentieth Century Communism*, Vol. 8 No. 8, 2015, pp27-29.
9. David Brandenberger, 'The Fate of Interwar Soviet Internationalism. A Case Study of the Editing of Stalin's 1938 *Short Course on the History of the ACP(b)*', *Revolutionary Russia*, Vol. 29 No. 1, 2016, pp13-4; David Brandenberger and Mikhail Zelenov, 'Stalin's Answer to the National Question. A Case Study on the Editing of the 1938 *Short Course*', *Slavic Review*, Vo. 73 No. 4, 2014, pp877-8.
10. On Stalin's attitude towards an understatement with Hitler, see Bernhard H. Bayerlein, 'Abschied von einem Mythos. Die UdSSR, die Komintern und der Antifaschismus 1930-1941', *Osteuropa*, Vol. 59 No. 7-8, 2009, pp144-5.
11. *Pravda*, 12 November 1918, p1.
12. *Pravda*, 11 November 1920, p1; *Pravda*, 12 November 1920, p1.
13. *Pravda*, 13 November 1921, p1.
14. *Pravda*, 7 November 1922, p3.
15. *Pravda*, 15 November 1922, p2.
16. *Pravda*, 14 November 1922, p1.
17. *Pravda*, 11 November 1924, pp1-2; 11 November 1925, p1; 9 November 1927, p1; 12 November 1927, p1; 12 November 1929, p1; 13 November 1929, p1; 10 November 1930, p1; 10 November 1931, p1.
18. On this, see Brooks, *op. cit.*, p65.
19. *Pravda*, 10 November 1931, p1.
20. *Pravda*, 10 November 1932, p4; 10 November 1933, p6; 10 November 1934, p5.
21. *Pravda*, 10 November 1936, p5.
22. *Ibid.*
23. Brandenberger, 'The Fate of Interwar Soviet Internationalism', p14.
24. *Pravda*, 10 November 1939, p4.
25. *Pravda*, 9 November 1939, p6.
26. Roger Moorhouse, *The Devils' Alliance: Hitler's Pact with Stalin, 1939-1941*, Basic Books: New York, 2014; Jan Tomasz Gross, *Revolution from Abroad. The Soviet Conquest of Poland's Western Ukraine and Western Belorussia*, Princeton University Press: Princeton, 2002.
27. Björn M. Felder, 'Stalinist National Bolshevism, Enemy Nations and Terror: Soviet Occupation of the Baltic States 1940-41', in Olaf Mertelsmann (ed.), *The Baltic States under Stalinist Rule*, Böhlau: Köln, 2016, pp13-26.

28. Ian Kershaw, *Hitler 1936-45: Nemesis*, Norton: New York, 2000, pp270-6; Ludolf Herbst, *Hitlers Charisma: Die Erfindung eines deutschen Messias*, Fischer: Frankfurt, 2010, pp210-17; Lars Pappert, *Der Hitlerputsch und seine Mythologisierung im Dritten Reich*, Ars Una: Neuried, 2001.
29. *Pravda*, 11 November 1939, p5.
30. *Pravda*, 8 November 1941, p4.
31. *Pravda*, 8 November 1941, p4; 8 November 1942, p1; 7 November 1943, p4; 11 November 1943, p1; 7 November 1944, p4; 8 November 1944, p1; 9 November 1944, p1; 11 November 1944, pp1-2.
32. *Pravda*, 8 November 1945, p2.
33. Peter Burke, 'Performing History: The Importance of Occasions', *Rethinking History*, Vol. 9 No. 1, 2005, pp38-41; John L. Austin, *How to Do Things with Words*, Clarendon Press: Cambridge, 1962, pp6-7.
34. Charles Gati, *Failed Illusions: Moscow, Washington, Budapest, and the 1956 Hungarian Revolt*, Stanford University Press: Stanford, 2006; Victor Sebestyen, *Twelve Days: The Story of the 1956 Hungarian Revolution*, Pantheon: New York, 2006.
35. *Pravda*, 8 November 1956, p4.
36. Asif A. Siddiqi, *Sputnik and the Soviet Space Challenge*, University of Florida Press: Gainesville, 2003; Deborah Cadbury, *Space Race. The Epic Battle Between America and the Soviet Union for Dominion of Space*, Harper Collins Publishers: New York, 2006, pp181-193.
37. *Pravda*, 8 November 1957, p2.
38. Martha Farner, *'Niemals vergessen!' Betroffene berichten über die Auswirkungen der Ungarn-Ereignisse 1956 in der Schweiz*, Limmat Verlag: Zürich, 1976, pp37-41.
39. *Pravda*, 8 November 1977, p4.
40. *Pravda*, 12 November 1971, p4; 14 November 1974, p4; 16 November 1977, p4; 14 November 1980, p4.
41. *Pravda,* 14 November 1980, p4.
42. Particularly during the NATO Operation 'Able Archer 83', from 2 to 11 November 1983, the two superpowers seemed to be at the abyss of a nuclear war: Peter Vincent Pry, *War Scare: Russia and America on the Nuclear Brink*, Greenwood: Westport, 1999, pp33-43.
43. *Pravda*, 7 November 1983, p7.
44. *Pravda*, 9 November 1983, p4.
45. *Pravda*, 8 November 1987, pp5-6; 9 November, pp4-11; 10 November, pp5-11; 11 November, pp6-10.

46. *Pravda*, 11 November 1987, p6.
47. *Pravda*, 8 November 1990, p4.
48. K. Ločmele, O. Procevska and V. Zelče, 'Celebrations, Commemorative Dates and Related Rituals: Soviet Experience, its Transformation and Contemporary Victory Day Celebrations in Russia and Latvia', in Nils Muižnieks (ed.), *The Geopolitics of History in Latvian-Russian Relations*, Academic Press of the University of Latvia: Riga, 2011, pp109-29.
49. *Pravda*, 8 November 2007, pp1-6.
50. www.pravda.ru/news/world/formerussr/belorussia/05-11-2016/1317441-bekarus-0/, 31 July 2017.

Notes on Contributors

Éric Aunoble is a senior lecturer and a senior research associate at the University of Geneva. His fields of interest are the revolutionary and the early Soviet periods, especially in Ukraine. His research tackles the questions of the mobilisation of the lower classes, and their involvement in party and state institutions; utopian practices; and the shaping of communism.

Kasper Braskén is Postdoctoral Researcher at Åbo Akademi University (Turku, Finland). He is a historian specialising in Germany, and the history of transnational social movements. Braskén has been visiting researcher at Zentrum für Zeithistorische Forschung (Potsdam 2008), Royal Holloway (London 2016), and Freie Universität Berlin (2014-2015; 2017-2019). He is author of the book *The International Workers' Relief, Communism, and Transnational Solidarity: Willi Münzenberg in Weimar Germany* (Palgrave Macmillan, 2015). Braskén is currently heading the 3-year Academy of Finland postdoctoral project 'Towards a Global History of Anti-Fascism: Transnational Civil Society Activism, International Organisations and Identity Politics Beyond Borders, 1922–1945'.

Anastasia Koukouna is a PhD student and teaching assistant at the University of Lausanne. She specialises in 1940s Greece, and the Greek communist movement. She is the author of the book *Surviving in Occupied Greece: The Swiss Red Cross Missions, 1942-1945 (2016, in Greek)*.

Daniel Kowalsky is a lecturer in European Studies at Queen's University, Belfast. He is the author of numerous books and articles on the civil war in Spain, including *La Unión Soviética y la guerra civil* *española* (Barcelona, Editorial Crítica, 2003), *Stalin and the Spanish Civil War* (New York: Columbia University Press, 2004), *History in Dispute*: *The Spanish Civil War* (Detroit: St. James Press, 2005) and, most recently, 'Operation X: Soviet Russia and the Spanish Civil War', in *Bulletin of Spanish Studies* 91: 1-2 (2014), pp 159-178.

André Liebich is honorary professor of international history and politics at the Graduate Institute, Geneva. He was previously professor of political science at the Université du Québec à Montréal. He received his PhD from Harvard University, and Doctor honoris causa from Babes-Bolyai University, Cluj-Napoca. He is author of 'From the Other Shore: Russian Social Democracy after 1921', *Harvard Historical Studies* 125 (Harvard University Press, 1997); pb 1999; Romanian translation, 2009; Fraenkel Prize. He edited (with Svetlana Yakimovich) *From Communism to Anti-Communism: Photographs from the Boris Souvarine Collection at the Graduate Institute, Geneva* (Graduate Institute Publications, 2016); and (with A. Nenarokov) *Men'sheviki v emigratsii: protokoly zagranichnoi delegatsii RSDRP*, vol. I 1922-1938, vol. II 1938-1951 (Rosspen, 2010).

Ottokar Luban was born in 1937 in Berlin. He studied history, psychology, education, political science, and special education at the College for Education and the Free University in Berlin (West). From 1960, he was a teacher in West Berlin, and is now retired. Since 1993, he has published on the history of labour movements, and has been voluntary secretary of the *International Rosa Luxemburg Society* since 1999.

Stephan Rindlisbacher is the recipient of a mobility grant from the *Swiss National Science Foundation*. From December 2016 to September 2019, he is conducting research on territorialisation processes in the early Soviet state in Moscow, Kiev, Tbilisi, Regensburg, and Basel. Prior to this, he worked as a teaching assistant at the Historical Department in Bern, where he wrote his PhD on the Russian radical movement in the late Tsarist Empire. He studied modern history, Slavic, and Islamic studies. He was educated across Europe at the Universities of Berne and Zagreb, and the State University of St Petersburg.

Index

A

Abramovitch Rein, Rafael, 161, 170, 172
Adler, Friedrich, 162
Akita, Ujaku, 9
Antonov-Ovseenko, Sofiia, 112, 115
Arafat, Yasser, 188
Arcas, Manuel Sánchez, 116-117
Armand, Ines, 42
Atatürk, Mustafa Kemal, 138, 182-183
Aksel'rod, Pavel Borisovich, 163,

B

Baden, Max von, 58-60
Bagaley, 39
Balabanova, Angelica, 65
Barbusse, Henri, 76-77, 91-92, 9
Barth, Emil, 61-63, 66
Bayerlein, Bernhard, 3
Bebel, August, 56
Bernstein, Eduard, 162
Blakytny, 40
Bourget, Paul, 34
Brezhnev, Leonid Ilyich, 18

Bukharin, Nikolai Ivanovich, 65, 79, 83-84, 91, 141
Burke, Peter, 186

C

Claudel Paul, 34

D

Däumig, Ernst, 62, 66, 70
Dahlem, Franz, 87
Dallin, David Iulevitch, 161, 167-168, 172
Dan, Fedor Illitch, 161-165, 167-172
David-Fox, Michael, 77
Dayan, Daniel, 117
Debord, Guy, 50
Dewey, John, 11
Dittmann, Wilhelm, 58
Dimitrov, Georgi Mikhaylovich, 109, 144
Dostoyevsky, Fyodor Mikhailovich, 107
Dovzhenko, Alexander Petrovich, 49
Dreiser, Theodore, 9
Duchêne, Gabrielle, 9

INDEX

Duncker, Hermann, 64-65
Duncker, Käte, 64

E

Ebert, Friedrich, 57-58, 60
Eisner, Kurt, 70
Einstein, Albert, 11
Eisenstein, Sergei Mikhailovich, 45, 48, 97, 121
Elser, Georg, 184
Engels, Friedrich, 168, 170

F

Fayet, Jean-François, 77
Filatova, 41
Fimmen, Edo, 97
Franco, Francisco, 110, 112
Fuchs, Eduard, 81-83

G

Glière, Reinhold Moritzevich, 16
Glinka, Mikhail Ivanovich, 107
Globa, Andrey, 34
Gogol, Nikolai Vasilievich, 107
Goldschmidt, Alfons, 88
Gomulka, Vladislav, 13
Gorbachev, Mikhail Sergeyevich, 190
Göring, Hermann, 184

H

Haase, Hugo, 57, 59, 63

Hanson, Richard, 184
Hilferding, Rudolf, 62
Hiller, Kurt, 88
Hindenburg, General von Paul, 56
Hirschfeld, Magnus, 88
Hitler, Adolf, 183-184
Hodann, Max, 95-96
Ho Chi Minh, 13
Hölz, Max, 93
Hoxha, Enver, 13

I

Istrati, Panaït, 9
Ivanov, 40

J

Joffe, Adolph, 63-65
Jogiches, Leo, 64
Jutteau, Kati, 118

K

Kadar, Janos, 13
Kalinin, Mikhail Ivanovich, 97, 121
Kamenev, Lev Borisovich, 166
Kameneva, Olga Davidovna, 81, 83
Karayorgis, Kostas, 142, 154
Katz, Elihu, 17
Kautsky, Karl, 62, 162-165
Kazantzakis, Nikos, 9
Kerensky, Alexander Fyodorovich, 80, 163

Khatchaturian, Aram Il'yich, 16
Khrennikov, Tikhon Nikolayevich, 16
Khrushchev, Nikita Sergeyevich, 13
Kyrkos, Michalis, 149
Kitsikis, Nikos, 148
Kolarov, 141.
Kollwitz, Käthe, 97
Konev, Ivan Stepanovich, General, 21
Kossior, Stanislav Vikentievitch, 40
Krupskaya, Nadejda Konstantinovna, 141
Kurella, Alfred, 84
Kviring, 38

L

Ledebour, Georg, 62-63
Liebknecht, Karl, 57-59, 61-62, 64
Linsingen, General von, 59
Lenin (Vladimir Ilyich Ulyanov), 44, 63, 64, 65, 68, 87, 108, 113, 118, 139, 163, 168, 180-182, 188, 191
Longuet, Jean, 136
Lunacharsky, Anatoly Vassilievitch, 6
Lukashenko, Aleksandr Grigoryevich, 191
Ludendorff, General, 56
Luxemburg, Rosa, 57-58, 64-65, 68

M

Manuilsky, Dmitri, 83-84, 109, 138
Mao Zedong, 13, 186
Martov, Iulii, 163-164, 167-170
Marx, Karl, 136, 163, 168, 171, 180
Mehring, Franz, 64
Mérimée, Prosper, 34
Meyer, Ernst, 64
Miller, Susanne, 67
Misiano, Francesco, 90
Molotov, Vyacheslav Mikhailovich, 79
Mosolov, Alexander Vasilyevich, 16
Müller, Richard, 61-62
Münzenberg, Willi, 10, 16, 77-88, 90, 94-96, 98-99
Muradeli, Vano, 16
Mursi, Fuad, 189-190
Myaskovsky, Nikolai Yakovlevich, 16

N

Nebolsin, 16
Nicolaevsky, Boris Ivanovich, 161, 170, 172-173
Nehru family, 9
Nora, Pierre, 178, 177

O

Osipovna, Lidia, 164, 172

INDEX

P

Papandreou, Georgios, 145
Paquet, Alfons, 88
Partsalidis, Dimitris, 142
Pascal, Pierre, 8
Petrovsky, 38
Pieck, Wilhelm, 186-187
Plekhanov, Georgi Valentinovich, 163
Pokko, 38
Polovtseva, Varvara N., 6
Porphyrogenis, Miltiadis, 152
Potresov, Alexander Nikolayevich, 163
Pouliopoulos, Pandelis, 141
Primakov, 40
Prokofiev, Sergei Sergeyevich, 16
Putin, Vladimir Vladimirovich, 191-192

R

Radek, Karl, 58
Rakovsky, Christian, 40
Ravich-Cherkassky, 38
Ribbentrop, Joachim von, 184
Rimsky-Korsakov, Nikolai Andreyevich, 107
Rolf, Malte, 178
Rolland, Romain, 9, 34
Roosevelt, Franklin D., 183
Roussos, Georgios, 140
Rubach, Mikhail, 39
Rykov, Alexeï Ivanovitch, 140, 170, 91
Ryappo, 38

S

Samoilova, Konkordiia Nikolavna, 42
Scheidemann, Philipp, 57-58
Serge, Victor, 139
Shah of Persia, 183
Shah of Afghanistan, 183
Shaw, George Bernard, 6, 11
Shostakovich, Dmitri Dmitriyevich, 16
Shvarts, Solomon Meerovitch, 161, 168
Siantos, Yorgis, 142
Siewert, Robert, 93
Sinclair, Upton, 11
Skrypnyk, 40
Stalin, Joseph Vissarionovich, 45, 93, 109-110, 114, 117, 119, 141, 163, 166, 168, 170, 182-183
Stein, Alexander, 62
Streuli, Hans, 187
Ströbel, Heinrich, 62
Studschka, Pjotr, 63
Stürgkh, Karl von, 162
Sun Yat-sen's widow, 9

T

Terek, A. (Olga Forsh's pseudonym), 34
Thälmann, Ernst, 87, 141
Theotokas, George, 146
Toller, Ernst, 9
Tolstoy, Count Lev Nikolayevich, 107

Trotsky, Leon, 6, 45, 91, 166, 177
Truman, Harry S., 185
Tsaldaris, Konstantinos, 151
Tsereteli, Irakli, 163
Tucholsky, Kurt, 88

U

Ulbricht, Walter, 13, 87

V

Vandervelde, Emile, 169
Vishniak, Mark Veniaminovich, 172
Volkenstein, Vladimir, 34
Voroshilov, Kliment Yefremovich, 92, 187
Vychinski, Andreï Ianouarievitch, 21

W

Walecki, Henryk, 65
Wells, Herbert George, 11

Y

Yavorsky, 40

Z

Zachariadis, Nikos, 142
Zatonsky, 40
Zetkin, Clara, 64, 81, 93
Zhivkov, Todor, 13
Zille, Heinrich, 88
Zinoviev, Grigori Evseïevitch, 166, 181